Transforming
Culture

Also by Sherwood Lingenfelter

Agents of Transformation: A Guide for Effective Cross-Cultural Ministry
The Deni of Western Brazil (with Gordon Koop)
Ministering Cross-Culturally: An Incarnational Model for Personal Relationships (with Marvin Mayers)
Yap: Political Leadership and Culture Change in an Island Society

Transforming Culture

A Challenge for Christian Mission

Second Edition

Sherwood Lingenfelter

Baker Books

A Division of Baker Book House Co
Grand Rapids, Michigan 49516

© 1998 by Sherwood Lingenfelter

Published by Baker Books
a division of Baker Book House Company
P.O. Box 6287, Grand Rapids, MI 49516-6287

Printed in the United States of America

Library of Congress Cataloging-in-Publication Data

Lingenfelter, Sherwood G.
    Transforming culture : a challenge for Christian mission / Sherwood Lingenfelter. — 2nd ed.
        p.   cm.
    Includes bibliographical references and indexes.
    ISBN 0-8010-2178-2 (pbk.)
    1. Missions—Anthropological aspects. 2. Intercultural communication. 3. Christianity and culture. I. Title.
    BV2063.L436   1998
    266—dc21

98-47736

For information about academic books, resources for Christian leaders, and all new releases available from Baker Book House, visit our web site:
http://www.bakerbooks.com

To

Dr. Judith E. Lingenfelter,
who for thirty-six years has been my partner in ministry,
my confidante and friend,
my colleague and professional adviser,
the mother of my children,
and my courageous, patient, enduring, and beloved wife.

For because of our faith, he has brought us into this place of highest privilege where we now stand, and we confidently and joyfully look forward to actually becoming all that God has had in mind for us to be. (Romans 5:1–2 LB)

Contents

Preface

The second edition of this book has been substantially revised. The first chapter reflects my growing understanding of the nature of culture as both our palace and prison. The second chapter is new and, I hope, much more accessible to the general reader than was its predecessor in the first edition. The middle chapters contain many of the same case studies of conflict, but much of the ethnographic description, which was burdensome to some readers, has been removed. I have omitted the final three chapters of the earlier edition and have written a new concluding chapter that focuses on the biblical challenge of being disciples of the Lord Jesus Christ, living as servants, shepherds, pilgrims, and strangers in a world of diverse and complex cultures.

The case studies presented in this volume are the result of field research that I have done in various settings around the world. I am deeply indebted to Louis and Lisa Shanks, Bob Mantel, and Jay and Beth Grant for their assistance and hospitality during the summer of 1986 as I visited and studied with them in African-American villages in the interior of Surinam. I am indebted to Gordon and Lois Koop, who were my hosts and coworkers for more than three months in 1977 in Brazil and without whose assistance I could not have written the material in this volume on the Deni Indians. The people of the Yap islands in the Federated States of Micronesia have allowed me to study their culture and to live among them for a period of nearly three years since 1967. I am especially indebted to Fran Defngin, Gabriel Ayin, Cyprian Mugunbey, and an elderly couple, Fithingrow and Marungweg, for their help on Yap culture. Many other Yapese men and women, from whom I have learned much, are too numerous to name here. I am also grateful to many pastor friends in southern California and my colleagues at Biola University, who have helped me to understand the people and culture of middle-class Americans as they relate to other minority groups in the southern California region.

I am especially indebted to people at Biola University for their support in preparing the manuscript. Wendy Walker and Peg Fosmark have typed drafts of the manuscript and contributed to all of the major revisions, including the preparation of the final manuscript for the publisher. I am especially grateful to Clyde Cook, the president of Biola University, who views scholarship as an important part of my work and has freed me to spend time in the summers on the mission field and to continue my scholarship as part of my administrative work as provost.

As is the case in the production of any book, I am deeply indebted to readers who have given me critical feedback. I am particularly grateful to students in my classes who have given me feedback from the first edition, colleagues Ed Harris and Steve Barber, and missionary friends from the Summer Institute of Linguistics in East Africa who have read some of the revised chapters and given helpful suggestions. I hope they find this edition a useful tool for training others.

1

Transferring or Transforming Culture?

Therefore, I urge you, brothers, in view of God's mercy, to offer your bodies as living sacrifices, holy and pleasing to God—this is your spiritual act of worship. Do not conform any longer to the pattern of this world, but be transformed by the renewing of your mind. Then you will be able to test and approve what God's will is—his good, pleasing and perfect will. (Rom. 12:1–2)

A few years ago some missionary colleagues and I attended a Sunday morning worship service in a large evangelical church in Cameroon's capital city of Yaounde. The African pastors led us in a familiar service, selecting songs from a standard evangelical hymnbook and preaching an inspiring, doctrinally sound message, given in English and translated into French. We missionaries, a few white faces in a sea of black believers, enjoyed the service thoroughly. As I walked away praising God, it suddenly occurred to me that this service was almost identical to those I had experienced in North America. Momentarily stunned, I wondered why I should feel as comfortable in Africa as if I were at home.

A week passed. I traveled to the interior in the northwest province of Cameroon, where I attended another worship service. There, the congregation sang unfamiliar music, the musicians played instruments dissonant and grating to my ears, and, while the pastor read from the King James Bible, he preached in a language foreign to me. Remembering my experience in Yaounde, I thanked God for the unique expression of worship in this African church. As I observed more carefully, however, I discovered many familiar things. These people had constructed a church building with gabled roof and steeple, arranged their benches in rows, and copied the platform and pulpit of a New England church. The men sat on one side and the women on the other, as was common in the home churches of early missionary pioneers. In the order of service only the language and the music were unfamiliar. As I reflected further on this African congregation, I discovered a structure nearly identical to that of the Baptist conferences with which I am familiar in the United States.

Why is it that in the process of establishing churches in non-Western nations we transfer our culture of the church? Can we find a biblical basis for this practice? Are missionaries planting biblically founded indigenous churches, or are they transferring their culture of Christianity to every nation of the world?

In Europe, Latin America, and Asia, I have found in every area a similar pattern of church planting. In North Borneo, the Anglican, evangelical, and Roman Catholic churches are all modeled on patterns brought by missionaries from various denominational and cultural backgrounds. It is difficult to find in the two-thirds world a truly indigenous church. Most churches reflect more the culture of the missionaries who planted them than they do the culture of the new believers.

Missionaries have succeeded in bringing a biblically informed worldview, but one that is thoroughly contaminated by their culture. Is it possible to bring a truly transforming gospel, or are we always limited to reproducing our own cultural reflection of Christianity wherever we carry the message?

Contextualization and Indigenization

The idea of contextualization is to frame the gospel message in language and communication forms appropriate and meaningful to the local culture and to focus the message upon crucial issues in the lives of the people. The contextualized indige-nous church is built upon culturally appropriate methods of evangelism; the process of discipling draws upon methods of instruction that are familiar and part of local traditions of learn-ing. The structural and political aspects of leadership are adapted from patterns inherent in national cultures rather than imported from denominational organizations in the home coun-tries of missionaries.

On an assignment with a mission in Surinam in 1986, I had the opportunity to observe such a contextualized indigenous church among Surinam Javanese. The pastor of this church was a Javanese man who for more than ten years had concentrated his ministry effort on evangelizing the youth among his people. Deeply discouraged to see these young men and women leave the fellowship of believers at the time of their marriages, he abandoned the youth ministry and began to concentrate on evan-gelizing adult men.

Through his contact with a Bible translation organization this pastor had gained a great appreciation for the Javanese lan-guage. He organized a band and wrote Christian songs using the familiar melodic pattern and appeal of Javanese music. Sat-urday evening became the prime time for evangelistic outreach; believers and unbelievers enjoyed a time of celebration in Christ. These evangelistic meetings offered food, fellowship, singing, and a fifteen-minute sharing of the gospel.

Seeing the response of people to these meetings, the pastor was inspired to launch a Sunday afternoon radio program. Drawing listeners through Javanese Christian music, inter-viewing men and women who were especially knowledgeable about Javanese culture, and focusing on a message of joy and hope, the pastor brought many listeners to respond to the gospel. He gave his home phone number and address to his radio lis-teners and received inquirers at any time of the day or night. Within the first year of the radio program more than eighty men, women, and children had received Christ through his ministry.

The organization of local churches growing out of this min-istry reflected Javanese values and priorities. The pastor delayed baptizing new believers until the whole family was ready, and he concentrated on discipling men. In turn, each family head discipled his wife and children. Worship services, emphasizing celebration and introducing unbelievers to the body of Christ, were held on Saturday evening. Small-group Bible studies were held in various locations on Sundays to disciple new believers.

The particular patterns developed in this Surinam Javanese church are a combination of Javanese and missionary strategies. The national pastor adapted the Christian faith to the unique needs of his own people. The outcome of his effort was a dynamic, growing church, as many Muslim men and women received the gospel and committed themselves to the Lord Jesus Christ.

In spite of the appeal of contextualization and indigenization for generating more effective church-planting ministries, these strategies are not without risk and potential abuse. Indigenization may lead to dead churches in the third and fourth generation of believers. Even in the New Testament we find Christians quickly defining the parameters of Christianity in terms of their own cultural limitations. The Book of Acts records an anti-Gentile mentality among Jewish converts. When Peter returned from his evangelistic trip to Joppa, he was immediately challenged by fellow believers who were critical of his eating with uncircumcised Gentiles (Acts 11:1–3). Some were not content with Peter's explanation, and later a faction of Jewish Christians proclaimed that unless converts did what believers did in Jerusalem, they could not be saved (Acts 15:1). When Paul arrived in Jerusalem late in his ministry, he discovered thousands of Jewish converts, all of them zealous for the law (Acts 21:20). The gospel had become completely conformed to Jewish culture, and the church had drifted to a particular, rather than a universal, vision of evangelism.

Gentile churches were no less susceptible to this indigenization problem. Before the death of John the apostle, five of the seven churches in Asia lost their vision, and two, Pergamum and Thyatira, had completely compromised the message of the gospel (Rev. 2–3). Both the indigenous Jewish churches and the indigenous Gentile churches succumbed to the pressures of culture and lost their vision and vitality.

How can we escape the dilemma of the dead indigenous church? Andrew Walls (1982, 97–99) contrasts the "indigenizing principle"—pressuring people into independence and isolation so that they conform to their own cultural surroundings at the price of detachment from the universal church—with the "pilgrim principle," which draws the church in the direction of the universals of the faith, rooted in obedience to Christ and the Scriptures. Jesus is the author of kingdom teaching and of the pilgrim principle, as recorded in his final hours with his disciples; Jesus prayed and asked the Father to protect his disciples and to keep them pilgrims, not of but in an evil world. In John 17:13–19 Jesus declares that they were not of the world, yet he concludes, "as you sent me into the world, I have sent them into the world." Walls suggests that pilgrim churches arise only when believers receive faithful instruction in the Word of God and respond with obedience as followers of Jesus Christ in a hostile world.

Contradiction: The Pilgrim and Indigenous Principles

The contradiction between the pilgrim principle, with its emphasis on the universal church and other-worldliness, and the indigenous principle, with its emphasis on self-support, self-government, and self-propagation in independent this-worldliness, is implicit in all church ministries. Indigenous churches, common in the history of the church, result from effective contextualization. While in their formation they serve as a powerful force for spreading the gospel, they may become a vehicle of compromise and death. The pilgrim principle, connecting local believers to the universal church with a vision for outreach to the world, provides a necessary counterbalance. Christians retain a commitment to bear witness to the world without becoming part of the world. The indigenous church without connection to the universal church and the Word dies. Entrenched in its own private vision of righteousness, it ceases to contextualize its message to needy people and loses vision and outreach.

What leads a local church to the privatization of the vision of Christ for the world? Members of every society hold a collective worldview and participate in structured social environments. Learning from parents and peers to accept and live in accord with certain values, beliefs, and procedures for action, they create a collective this-worldliness, which becomes a prison of disobedience. So entangled, they live a life of conformity to social images that are in conflict with God's purpose for humanity. Paul suggests that human beings are in a prison, a cell of disobedience: "God has imprisoned all human beings in their own disobedience only to show mercy to them all" (Rom. 11:30–32 NJB). In Galatians 3:22, paraphrasing Psalm 14:1–3, he observes that "the whole world is a prisoner of sin." God has penned up all people in their self-created cells of culture, including Jew and Gentile, pagan and missionary.

This view of culture is at odds with the perspective of earlier missiologists. Charles H. Kraft and Marvin K. Mayers, working from the viewpoint that cultures are integrated, functioning systems, argue that culture is a neutral vehicle through which God communicates to human beings. Kraft (1981, 113) states that "culture consists of forms, functions, meanings, and usage . . . a kind of road map made up of various forms designed to get people where they need to go. These forms and the functions they are intended to serve are seen, with few exceptions, as neutral with respect to the interaction between God and man. Cultural patterning, organizing, and structuring of life . . . are not seen as inherently evil or good in themselves." Mayers (1987, 251) suggests that "it is entirely possible that the gospel can enter a life and a society without change being called for."

In this volume I reject the notion that culture or worldview is neutral. Analogies such as Kraft's map or "a tool for communication and interaction" (Lingenfelter and Mayers 1986, 122) are inadequate to capture the pervasive presence of sin in the lives and thought of human beings. Using the analogy of a tool, we can say culture is more like a slot machine found in Las Vegas's gambling casinos than a wrench or a screwdriver. Culture, like a slot machine, is programmed to ensure that those who hold power win and the common players lose; when or if the organized agenda is violated, people frequently resort to violence to reestablish their programmed advantage. Every cultural system brokers power to its members, although the power advantage may be held by either individuals or groups. The structures and organizations of cultures are not neutral; people define and structure their relationships with others to protect their personal or group interests and to sustain or gain advantage over others with whom they compete. Video games provide better analogies to culture than does Kraft's map, because they reflect the various power advantages, access to survival resources, and hostile opposition that typify cultural systems.

Culture is created and contaminated by human beings; culture is the pen of disobedience from which freedom is possible only through the gospel. H. Richard Niebuhr (1951, 165) elucidates how the writings of Paul address this issue, portraying Christ in the role of "the judge of culture and the redeemer to Christian culture." Culture seeks to maintain social control through its rules, norms, and sanctions for behavior, and thus it limits certain kinds of sinful or deviant behavior. Yet the rules of culture reflect a natural knowledge of God (Rom. 2:14–15) that serves to expose sin rather than bring people to righteousness.

The gospel, in contrast, liberates men and women from the cell of disobedience. Peter writes, "You were redeemed from the empty way of life handed down to you from your forefathers . . . with the precious blood of Christ" (1 Peter 1:18–19). The gospel brings a contradictory message to the peoples of the world, challenging their social order and beliefs. Peter again clarifies, "But you are a chosen people, a royal priesthood, a holy nation, a people belonging to God, that you may declare the praises of him who called you out of darkness into his wonderful light. Once you were not a people, but now you are the people of God" (1 Peter 2:9–10).

The Scriptures show clearly that Jesus challenged the accepted society and worldview. Although he was living as a Jew in the Jewish world, he shattered that world with his preaching and teaching. His good news brought conflict and change. People in Judea and Samaria hated him and plotted to kill him because he challenged their system. They did everything they could to destroy Jesus and his followers.

Likewise, when believers carried the gospel into the Greco-Roman world, they overturned traditional beliefs and provoked social conflict. The Greeks in Ephesus, furious at Paul's message because it was bad for business, rioted against him. When the gospel challenges with power any worldview, unbelievers react to defend their view and may inflict great distress upon Christians.

Paul Hiebert (1985) argues that Christianity provides a new hermeneutic for cultural living. Every culture and every person must change in light of a new perspective—Jesus Christ, crucified, risen, and exalted. Jesus came to save not cultures but people, and he came to transform them into his likeness. But whole cultures *will not* be transformed! The opposite is true. Church and mission history suggests that the larger culture neutralizes the church of Jesus Christ, as is often evident in the third or fourth generation of its new or renewed existence.

Perhaps Christians have accepted a common notion that God has a system that includes particular kinds of behaviors, institutions, and personality traits. Luther, Calvin, Wesley, and other leaders of Reformation theologies and institutions proclaimed that their version of the church most closely represented the system called for in Scripture. They articulated how the kingdom teaching of Christ should be expressed in their social and cultural worlds. While church leaders have not always seen eye to eye on the relationship of the gospel and culture (Niebuhr 1951), they have all struggled with corruption in culture and sought ways to purify the church from that corruption. In every case, however, in just a few generations the Reformation churches reflect more the social worlds of Germany, Switzerland, and England than a dynamic, universally oriented, culture-transforming church.

Transformation is neither bridging from one system to another nor transferring a Christian system to another place and people. Rather, transformation means a new hermeneutic—a redefinition, a reintegration of the lives of God's people (the church) within the system in which they find themselves living and working. Jesus said, "My kingdom is not of this world" (John 18:36). He thus denied the existence of a Christian sociopolitical system but called for the transformation of his disciples' thinking and social relationships with others.

The argument of this book is that the social and cultural systems of a missionary and a local, indigenous community exert powerful pressure on new believers and churches, pressure to conform to habitual standards, values, and practices. Christians cannot live apart from the social games of the church or the wider society, and therefore they are subject to these unrelenting forces. Further, Christian leaders teach and practice standards and values that are inextricably intertwined with those of their social world.

Nevertheless, the gospel may become a significant powerful force in the continuous restructuring of any social environment and worldview. As believers become mature in their faith, their interests reflect more and more those of the Lord Jesus Christ. Therefore Christians will experience tension and contradiction with old patterns of self-interest and greed, provoking them to contradict old social rules and judge many inadequate as they attempt to imitate the person of Christ in their lives and work. As believers increasingly obey the truth of the gospel, they will discover new ways of managing resources and relationships.

Synthesis: Prisons, Pilgrims, and Transformation

How can Christian workers avoid transferring their culture and nurture maturing, indigenous churches that are committed to evangelism and the transformation of their local culture as disciples of the Lord Jesus Christ? The solution presented in the chapters that follow is similar to that presented by Mayers (1987, 247–60) in his combination of biblical absolutism and cultural relativism. We agree on the truth and authority of Scripture and on the pluralism that characterizes cultures and affects the ministry enterprise. We differ in our view of culture and worldview: Mayers has a high and neutral view of culture, while the view of culture presented here is a low view, that of culture inextricably infected by sin.

The first task is understanding our prison and the cultural prisons of others. The notion of a prison of disobedience is repulsive to many. We often picture a prison as a medieval dungeon, deep underground in a stone castle, with bars, clanking iron doors, and a small trapdoor through which the keeper thrusts our daily rations of moldy bread and water. No wonder readers resist this conceptualization of culture. Perhaps a different illustration will help. A beautiful walled park in the center of Seoul, Korea, contains the homes, gardens, and servants' quarters of the king and royal family of Korea. During the nineteenth century the king and his family occupied this famous residence, the

Palace of the Secret Garden. Because of his extremely high status, custom declared that the king could not leave the palace grounds; he was in fact a prisoner in his palace. However, life within the walls was magnificent. He enjoyed the most beautifully furnished, heated, and decorated living quarters in Korea. He had household servants to care for every need. He enjoyed a beautiful garden and pond where the finest scholars, poets, and artists in Korea came to do their work. The only catch: he was a political prisoner, unable to see and experience the outside world. To compensate for this deprivation, he had a second palace built on the back of the palace grounds. This palace, decorated in black and white, gave the king the illusion of what it was like to live in the "commoner world" outside of the palace walls. But it was only an illusion; he lived in his prison unaware of the pain, poverty, and freedom of the life of a commoner.

The Gospels recount the story of how Satan tempted the Lord Jesus at the beginning of his ministry. In the temptation to seek power, Satan took Jesus to a high place and "showed him in an instant all the kingdoms of the world. And he said to him, 'I will give you all their authority and splendor, for it has been given to me, and I can give it to anyone I want to. So if you worship me, it will all be yours'" (Luke 4:5–7). The point of this story for us is that the kingdoms of the world are splendid, and they belong to Satan. Jesus later declared, "my kingdom is not of this world" (John 18:36).

Our cultural palaces are our prisons; in them we find comfort, security, meaning, and relationships. Yet the wall of culture restricts our freedom and sets barriers between us and others of different ethnic origin. The splendid kingdoms of history and the nation states of the present are many and diverse, and they have been given to Satan. Culture, economy, and state are his to rule as God allows. The church is called out, the people of God, to live in a world of many cultures as "strangers and pilgrims" (1 Peter 2:11 KJV).

The life of the pilgrim is unsettled; no single culture is adequate, settling down is temporary, and accommodation to culture is for a higher purpose. Peter tells us to "live such good lives among the pagans that, though they accuse you of doing wrong, they may see your good deeds and glorify God on the day he visits us" (1 Peter 2:12). When we enter another culture we must examine the life and beliefs of those people; we must learn how to live good lives according to their standards; we must live in submission to their authorities; we must discover their significant questions; and we must search the Scriptures to find biblical answers to their questions and needs, recognizing the limitations of our own views.

To live as pilgrims and make pilgrim disciples, we must learn how to "live as free men . . . servants of God" and at the same time live in submission to "every authority instituted among men" (1 Peter 2:13–16). How do we achieve both freedom and submission? We cannot get out of prison until we can see clearly the walls, the gates, and the gatekeepers. The purpose of this book is to help the reader comprehend the dimensions of our cultural prisons and discover some of the biblical keys that will allow us to unlock the chains of our cultural habits and the gates to our cultural walls. These same perspectives will enable us to share our experience of freedom with others and lead them in the journey of becoming followers of Jesus Christ.

In the pages that follow the cross-cultural worker—evangelist, church planter, teacher, nurse, community developer, linguist, literacy worker, translator—will discover the social roots of interpersonal conflicts endemic to living and working with people of different cultural and social heritages. When we carefully examine ourselves, we shall be forced to admit that more often than not we conform theology to practice; we perceive the kingdom of God on earth in our own cultural terms.

Only by recognizing that cultural blindness is the rule, not the exception, and that our philosophies are our windows onto the world, can we free our fellowship and our theology from the bondage of our cultural philosophies and worldview. We must look through multiple windows if we are to genuinely apprehend the transforming power of the gospel and apply kingdom principles interculturally. Each believer sees through a glass, narrow and constraining, but together as disciples with differing perspectives, we can begin to comprehend the wider impact of the Scripture in a pluralistic world.

Of course, escape from our cultural prison is never total until we are with Christ. Because we are born into a social world, socialized into its language and thought, we will always be blinded by its sin. While this book may enable the reader to see more clearly a particular social chain, escape from the prison of disobedience is a work of grace, empowered through the Spirit in the body of Christ. That is why we need other believers, redeemed and being transformed in their prisons, to help us understand how God's Word contradicts our thinking and our way of life. Together we may teach one another about the sources of our mutual blindness.

2
A Model for Analysis of Social Order

An American missionary in the Caroline Islands in the western Pacific chanced upon a group of children and teenagers playing a ball game. Standing in a tight circle, they took turns hitting a ball into the air, bouncing it randomly around and across the circle. After watching for a time, the missionary asked one of the players, "How do you determine who wins in this game?" The Carolinian laughed as he replied, "No one wins; the object of the game is to keep the ball in the air. We play together to keep the ball flying as long as possible."

Americans have a similar game, volleyball. However, in volleyball two teams compete with each other to keep the ball in the air, and each team tries its best to cause the other team to fail in this task. The American game has many rules, such as boundaries of play, number of players, how many times a person and a team can hit the ball, hitting the ball over a net, and not touching the net. The game always ends with one team the victor.

These two games reflect some key assumptions about the social worlds of the players. In the Caroline Islands people place high value on working together in community. They try hard to work together and to moderate their personal performance so they do not stand out among the others in the community. They avoid win/lose situations in their social life as well as in their social games. Working from these social assumptions, they believe that the most important goal in work and play is to keep everybody participating and to make sure that every person in the group succeeds.

While Americans clearly believe in teamwork, they have a hard time imagining a game without a winner and a loser. Baseball, basketball, football, soccer, hockey, and volleyball all require that one team win and the other lose. In most of these games the rules require that the players continue to play until a tie score is broken and one team clearly emerges as a winner. In addition the social organization of these games is often much more complex than that of the ball game in the Carolines. Americans have managers, coaches, assistant coaches, team captains, specialized performance roles for the players, and a cadre of substitute players who relieve the starters when they tire or fail to play effectively. Further, the rules of the game frequently prescribe specific roles and play action for each member of a team. In football, a lineman may not go downfield until after the ball is thrown, and a back may move sideways but not forward until the ball is snapped.

Both Americans and Carolinians know that people play other kinds of games. Foot racing is a common activity among Carolinian boys. Girls often play the string game of cat and the cradle. However, the Carolinians play these individual performance games differently than do their American counterparts. For example, in American high schools individual performers in track and field do everything in their power to excel against their peers and to set new performance records for their school, conference, and state. And the schools keep careful records of individual performance so that young athletes have personal and public standards against which to measure their performance.

Carolinian athletes also want to win their races, but they are careful about how they do it. The runner in front always looks back to see how far he is leading his peers. If he is too far ahead, he will slow down so that others do not get discouraged and quit running. His goal is to win, but only by a step, so that he does not offend the other runners by showing off his speed. A few years ago I was watching a baseball game on the Carolinian island of Yap. In the fourth inning the team at bat scored twelve runs. When the twelfth run crossed the plate, the team in the field walked off in utter humiliation, and the game ended. Further, the spectators ridiculed the winners for showing off at the expense of the other team.

The structure of play in our cultures follows closely the structure of the more serious social games by which we order our public and private lives. As you reflect on the preceding illustrations, you can identify some of the deeper social themes of American and Carolinian culture. Carolinian individuals must submit to group goals and restrain their personal performance so that others in their communities do not lose honor or respect. American individuals measure their personal performance, as well as their team performance, and they prize winning on both fronts. For sports such as baseball, teams keep personal as well as team statistics, and players compete aggressively for the best individual statistics. For many players, personal failure hurts more than team failure. The public demands success for both the team and the individual players, and they ridicule failure. Americans carry similar values and priorities into their government, businesses, universities, and even their churches.

The Structure of Social Games

Social anthropologist Mary Douglas (1982, 190) has identified two social factors, grid and group, that enable us to decipher the unique features of a social game and understand its social order. Grid and group identify the two distinctive dimensions of social life found in every social game.

We use grid to describe the different ways in which people define the place and role of individuals in a game or a social activity. For example, on a volleyball team every player performs every skill at every position. While each individual will have strengths and weaknesses, every player must serve, play the net, and rotate through the positions on the court. Baseball, in contrast, has nine distinctive positions of play, and each player is a specialist. Pitchers only pitch, catchers only catch, and the first, second, and third basemen play only these specific positions.

Should a coach ask a player to change position, the player often refuses, unless the only other choice is not to play at all. Volleyball is a weak grid social game, with a few positions that everyone plays. Baseball is a strong grid social game, with many sharply defined positions and one or two persons skilled and trained to fill each position on the team.

We use group to describe the different ways in which people define the identity and relationships of members of a team, extended family, or community. To illustrate this principle we may compare the difference between the Claysburg High School baseball team where my father played and the Los Angeles Dodgers, a professional baseball team. To become a member of the Claysburg High School baseball team my dad lived in the community, enrolled in the high school, and performed successfully as a student. Several of his brothers, as well as cousins and nephews, had played on the team, so playing was a family affair. Members of his family came to watch the games and applaud his success or console his failure. The team had strong rivalries with other local schools, and my dad and his teammates represented not only their school but also the community and their families. Even after he graduated from high school, he kept his strong loyalty to the team and went back to root for the young players who followed him, playing against the rival schools. In contrast, members of the Los Angeles Dodgers gain their position by an invitation of the owners to try out, and if they demonstrate the required skill, the owner may offer the player a contract. Players, coming from all over the nation and the world, negotiate their contracts through professional agents, who seek the best financial terms possible for a specified number of years. When the period of the contract ends, a player negotiates with the owner of any professional team interested in bidding for his services. The Claysburg High School baseball team has a much more complex group identity than do the Los Angeles Dodgers. When group identity is complex, members often feel stronger loyalty to one another and have more obligations for mutual support. The Dodgers have a simplex group identity; that is, the player/owner contract. Under these circumstances players seek their own best interests, which are often, but not always, served by team loyalty and mutual support.

The Concept of Grid

The idea of grid focuses on how people in a social game categorize and constrain individual players by distinctive positions and roles. The more numerous and specialized the positions of players and the greater the performance restriction (pitchers only pitch), the stronger the grid. More social distinctions usually imply more sharply defined expectations and social rules. The larger the number of rules, the greater the constraints upon individuals in the structuring of social relationships; managers do not socialize with players, and presidents of companies do not socialize with laborers.

In a weak grid social game, players make few social distinctions among their members. The players keeping the ball in the air in the Caroline Islands made no distinction between boys and girls or older and younger players. All played equally, and all shared in the joy and distress of the game. In other weak grid games, such as American volleyball, members may identify individuals who have particular skills that are respected, or they may identify individuals as leaders while expecting each member to play all positions.

Social games characterized by weak grid emphasize the unique value of individuals within an open, competitive environment. People emphasize fair competition, and each individual is valued for personal history and character strengths rather than by particular role distinctions. Since most individuals have potential access to all of the roles available, no particular role is given distinctive value over other ones.

In a strong grid social game, people often order the player positions in a hierarchy with a few major players at the top and many others in the middle and on the bottom. The players at the top of the hierarchy have uniquely defined value and power. The baseball pitcher who wins twenty games or the batter who hits forty home runs gets paid far more than does the manager of the team, and these players have much greater influence than do middle-level players. The president of a major corporation earns millions more annually than does a middle manager or a production line worker and has great power over decisions of the company. Generally such roles are limited to a small number of individuals within the total social environment.

In contrast, the middle- and lower-level players have much less autonomy and are constrained by the hierarchy and rules regulating their positions. For example, within a university, department chairs and faculty members occupy middle or lower positions in the hierarchy. While these people are valued within the university, individual players often feel constrained by the power structure above them. Each person occupies a particular niche and plays a role that on the surface seems isolated and unconnected with others. The specialist in Victorian literature may have no one other than students with whom to discuss that specialty. As a consequence, that faculty member feels isolated and alone, enjoying the support of peers only at one or two yearly professional meetings of other Victorian specialists.

Grid should not be confused with the traditional anthropological and sociological concepts of achieved and ascribed status. Strong grid social games may include both achieved and ascribed status positions. For example, in baseball and a university, most players have achieved status positions. Players must earn high batting or pitching averages or doctoral degrees and promotions to advance within the hierarchy. Yet, playing for the New York Yankees or the Los Angeles Dodgers has an ascribed status not given to players for the Texas Rangers or the Seattle Mariners. In the university a professor with a doctoral degree from Harvard University has an ascribed status not granted to a professor with a similar degree from Ohio State University, and access to a faculty position in any university is easier for the Harvard graduate than it is for the Ohio State graduate.

The Concept of Group

The idea of group is more familiar to us, yet the distinction between weak and strong group is often difficult to grasp. First, let us distinguish social group from social identity. Social identities—such as American versus Canadian or Christian versus Muslim—are categories by which individuals and groups define themselves in opposition to others, without any necessary connection between people in the same category. Social group, however, defines a team or a collective to which individuals belong, having specific criteria of membership, such as the Los Angeles

Dodgers, Wycliffe Bible Translators, or the First Baptist Church
of Portland.

When people form weak groups, the social glue that holds
the group together is usually limited to a common identity and
some mutual interests and activities. For example, the Vineyard churches in southern California have no members, only
attenders. To associate with the church, a person attends. Levels of participation vary; some people only attend, others attend
and give financial support, others participate in ministries, and
still others take leadership responsibility. The level of participation rests solely upon the attenders' interest and personal
commitment.

A church or a team that values strong group commitment
places higher demands upon the members and gives them priv-
ileged access to group benefits. First, strong group games make
membership a selective and difficult process. We have already
noted how a high school baseball team places many more group
requirements on a player than does a professional baseball team.
The Grace Brethren church to which I belong provides a modest contrast to the Vineyard. Attenders are welcome, but they
are not members. To become a member, an attender must complete a membership class, be baptized by immersion (three times
forward), and sign a statement supporting the doctrines, ordi-
nances, and ministries of the church.

Second, strong group games grant members privileges denied
to nonmembers. In my church only members may vote on
church matters and take leadership roles in church ministries.
Yet attenders may enjoy all the benefits of church programs and
ministries, including taking communion; members exclude them
only from formal decision making and leadership. The exclusive Plymouth Brethren have stronger group commitments than
do the Grace Brethren; they practice closed communion, allow-
ing only members to participate. The Plymouth Brethren draw
sharper boundaries between insiders and outsiders and exclude
outsiders from all of the core activities of the church.

In a weak group social game, such as the Vineyard, people
create ministry teams, but these ministry teams are often temporary and players have short-term commitments. Players tend
to focus on activities rather than long-term corporate objectives,
and their allegiance to the ministry team fluctuates and changes.

Usually these ministry teams form for a particular period of time and to meet a certain objective. Once the objective is met and the time has passed, the members scatter, rarely if ever to reunite as a ministry team.

The strong group social game involves relationships invested with social and symbolic meaning. The elder board in a Plymouth Brethren assembly is based upon high trust and long-term relationships rather than upon practical, short-term objectives. Membership involves spiritual and ministry qualifications judged over a long period of personal intimacy and social meaning. The elders cannot conduct business without first giving attention to the spiritual and social constraints of the assembly. A strong group social environment is characterized by enduring relationships and commitments to group goals and procedures. The group has a life that lasts beyond that of its individual members and perpetuates its resources and meanings over a much longer period of time. The goal of group interaction is to perpetuate the life of the group rather than the life of its individual members.

Five Prototype Social Games

Working from the variables of grid and group, there are five, and only five, prototypes from which people construct their social games (fig. 2.1). A prototype is a model, exemplary in its form, that allows us to observe, analyze, and classify the wonderfully complex diversity that characterizes human social life. Following Thompson, Ellis, and Wildavsky (1990), I shall name these prototypes the individualist, authoritarian, hierarchist, egalitarian, and autonomy games. The autonomy game of total self-reliance is played by the hermit, who drops out of society and deplores the social constraints of grid and group (zero grid, zero group). The individualist game promotes the freedom of individuals, open competition, and the right of individuals to determine their own rules and way of life in loose cooperation with others. The authoritarian game emphasizes the power and authority of hierarchy, embracing strong grid with only limited social constraints of group accountability. The hierarchist game combines the authority of hierarchy with the accountability of group. The egalitarian game emphasizes equal access to power and responsibility and strong group consensus for decisions, while it deplores hierarchy and upholds equity within the group.

Figure 2.1
Five Prototype Social Games

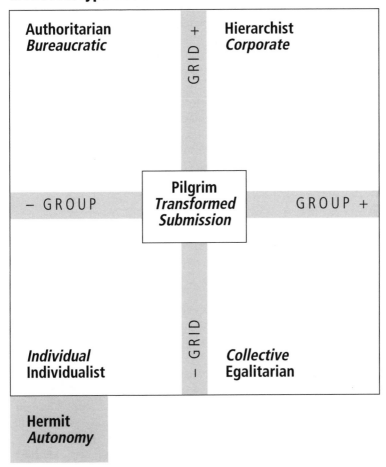

Each of these prototypes is available in any society, and most societies utilize several if not all of these games in some aspect of their social life. The differences in cultures and societies are the result of a complex blending of two or more of these social games with language, economic systems, and a worldview that blends social values with religion and a cultural philosophy of life. For the purpose of illustration, I will show how American Christians utilize each of these prototype games to order their peculiar expression of church and faith.

The Vineyard Fellowship, originating in southern California, is one of several examples of churches organized around the individualist social game prototype (others include Calvary chapels and Christian churches). We have already seen how the Vineyard rejects the notion of membership, drawing people into its fellowship through a strong experience of personal and collective worship and power ministry to meet felt needs for healing and a prophetic personal relationship with God. The Vineyard also rejects formal organization and structured leadership. Leaders are called by God to serve the congregation or the community. Any and every attender should expect some call to service, and it is their individual responsibility to respond. An attender is as likely as a staff member to receive a prophetic message from the Lord. Leaders emerge from prolonged and effective service to the church, demonstrating spiritual gifts and effective ministry. Churches have boards to meet the requirements of state law, but the board's role is symbolic rather than structural.

The Orthodox church in America participates in a church tradition and structure that is authoritarian in its social game. The glue that holds this and other archdioceses of the Orthodox church together is a commitment to Orthodox doctrine, liturgy, tradition, and bureaucracy. Each local church follows an exact church calendar and liturgy for each Sunday of the year and for special holy days such as Pentecost, Ascension, and many others. The organization of the archdiocese follows a carefully defined traditional authority structure. Each congregation has a priest who oversees a clearly defined structure of lay leadership. Communion is closed, so that only members may partake, yet this rule follows from the chain of command hierarchy rather than the strength of group identity. While some congregations may have a strong group community, the church functions well without it. The ecclesiastical rule, in which the bishops are shepherds and teachers, sustains the doctrinal commitments, tradition, identity, and function of the church. Members may come to the church for the service and have no other contact or commitment to one another. Their spiritual life and ministry are focused upward through the priest and the ruling structure of the church.

While many denominations operate as variations on the hierarchist social game, the Presbyterian churches exemplify a balanced blending of strong grid and strong group. Each local church has a board of elders and a board of deacons. The elders constitute the session of the church, which is its ruling body. The pastor is a member of the elder board but votes only to break a tie vote. The churches participate in county (presbytery), state (synod), and national (general assembly) levels of organization, electing representatives for each level. Members elect their leaders and hold them accountable through a regular process of review and reelection. Pastors, elders, and deacons serve their congregations and sessions in specialist roles, defined by either the local session or the presbytery. While some rotation through these positions is required, only those who have met the qualifications for service are elected. Members of a church may participate in the elections and governing structure; only members may receive financial support for a church-related ministry.

The Plymouth Brethren assemblies, originating in the British Isles, exemplify the egalitarian social game. As we have observed, a person gains membership in an assembly by meeting rigorous doctrinal and faith requirements. The communion service is the worship meeting in an assembly, and it is carefully distinguished from the ministry meeting that usually follows. The exclusive Plymouth Brethren practice closed communion, while open assemblies allow outsiders who are believers to participate. The ministry meeting that follows communion includes attenders and children of members who are not yet able to attend the communion service. Brethren assemblies generally do not have pastors or paid staff; elders in the assembly preach on Sundays, as the spirit of the Lord leads them, and most if not all elders take their turn. Eldership is open to every man in the assembly who meets the group's rigorous spiritual, service, and doctrinal expectations. Members exercise their spiritual gifts and serve the congregation as teachers, youth workers, and evangelists. However, members rotate through all of the responsibilities of service in the assembly.

Many Americans who in surveys claim to be born-again Christians do not attend any church or associate with any group of believers. They have chosen the autonomy game as it relates to their Christian faith. They are for all practical purposes Christian "hermits." They accept no authority apart from their own. They may listen to Christian broadcasting, read Christian literature, and have a life of private worship and prayer. Yet they choose to remain apart from other Christians and local churches. They may have other social relationships and play other social games in their work or family life. They have chosen to make their faith a private affair and live apart, autonomous in religious life.

Cultural Bias

In chapter 1 we asked the question, Why is it that in the process of establishing churches in non-Western nations we transfer our culture of the church? We are at a point where we can begin to answer this question. The social games that we play are much more than games. They reflect a particular bias that we have about the best and right way to live our collective life of faith. If we could take the time to examine the theological underpinnings of each of the churches described, we would find careful biblical and theological justification for each particular social expression of the church. Every tradition founds its church practice upon a theological rationale that can be supported from Holy Writ. Are all the others blind to what Scripture really says, and do we alone have the truth? Or are we indeed all in prisons of disobedience?

In 1979 my family spent a year living on the island of Yap in the western Caroline Islands. My eight-year-old son, Joel, in the stress of his first cross-cultural experience, refused to leave the house to play in the village. When I asked why, he expressed great indignation and anger: "Dad! These kids don't know how to play!" I was astonished and replied that I saw them playing all the time. To which he replied, "They don't know how to play RIGHT." Joel had intuitively grasped a fundamental truth about human social life; we can tolerate one and only one of the prototype games in any area of significant meaning in our lives. Because our faith is such a significant part of our life experience, we, like Joel, know only one way to do it right.

Each of the social games has far-reaching implications for our life and worldview. If we adopt the individualist game, we cannot tolerate the coercion of hierarchy or group. We see our relationship to God as direct and personal; no one or no group can mediate that for us. If we adopt the egalitarian game, there is only one truth, and we have it. Anyone who disagrees is a threat to the whole group. We must work to insure that what we collectively believe is true and protect the purity of our faith by excluding anyone who disagrees.

When we adopt the hierarchist game, our level of tolerance increases significantly. Leadership and unity are more important than conformity on lesser doctrinal issues. Yet revelation is not open to everyone, as in the individualist and egalitarian games. Some persons have greater gifts of interpretation, teaching, and preaching. We look to great preachers, scholars, and teachers to define the parameters of our faith and practice, yet within accepted group parameters. For authoritarians anything that challenges tradition and hierarchy is out of bounds. God reveals himself through the apostles, the Scriptures, and the great church councils that have considered most if not all of the central theological issues and have rendered their decision. Leaders explain and interpret those decisions for the faithful, and no further revelation occurs apart from the church.

The structure of a social game leads the participants to adopt a related set of assumptions and values that are elaborated in their worldview. We call these values and assumptions *cultural bias*. Each social game has a peculiar cultural bias, and only one bias can be right. Our preferences for social order create preferences for church structure, theology, and worship. If we are individualists, we prefer our own interpretation of Scripture. If we are egalitarian, we together hold the correct view. If we are hierarchist, we trust experts, and if we are authoritarian, only the priest and the church can be trusted to lead us to truth.

These deep assumptions and priorities for social and church life led Presbyterian missionaries to establish churches in Korea and West Africa identical to their home churches in America. However, they are not alone. Baptist, Anglican, Brethren, and

Vineyard missionaries replicate their home churches in every corner of the world. They do so because they cannot imagine, as my son could not imagine, that any other way could be right. Their church life at home is a synthesis of their social game, theology, faith, and practice. God has met them in a personal way through that experience, and their cultural bias leads them to assume their way is the best if not the only viable one.

The Christian Pilgrim Lifestyle

While the Scripture does not refer directly to social game or cultural bias, it does speak directly about the character and the quality of our personal, social, and spiritual life and about the tension between living in the unnatural state of separation from God and the restoration to the fullness of life with God through Christ. Although a complete escape from cultural bias is impossible while we live in the flesh of the body and in social relationships, the Spirit-filled Christian has the power through Jesus Christ to live with a significant degree of freedom.

The Book of Ephesians (2:1–3) draws graphic contrast between life in and apart from Christ. Paul describes the human condition apart from Christ as "dead in your transgressions and sins . . . when you followed the ways of this world and . . . the spirit who is now at work in those who are disobedient." The world encompasses the three significant, independent variables of culture—knowledge, social games, and economic systems. People in the unnatural state of separation from God are guided primarily by the knowledge of their cultural system, the social and political order of their society, and the local and world economies that organize human production and material life. Paul connects the course of this world with the "ruler of the kingdom of the air." The world systems are linked spiritually to the prince of darkness. Not only do we as individuals live in these systems, but also Paul notes that we do so "indulging the desires of the flesh and of the mind" (Eph. 2:3 NASB). As individuals we play out the sin that is part of our life histories and personalities.

The wonderful news of the gospel is that, while we were once dead, "God, who is rich in mercy, made us alive with Christ"

(Eph. 2:4). Paul characterizes the believer as a "new creation" (2 Cor. 5:17) restored in relationship with God, created anew for a life of good works in the same world that once held the person in slavery. Peter employs several metaphors to capture the essence of this new life—obedient children, living stones, a spiritual house, a people belonging to God. Yet Peter's most compelling metaphor is the one he uses to teach believers how to continue to live in the world. "Dear friends, I urge you, as aliens and strangers in the world, to abstain from sinful desires, which war against your soul. Live such good lives among the pagans that, though they accuse you of doing wrong, they may see your good deeds and glorify God on the day he visits us" (1 Peter 2:11–12). The King James translation of this text refers to believers as pilgrims—people who continue their journey in the world but live as aliens, no longer invested in the agendas of the dead.

Throughout this book we will continually return to the metaphor of the pilgrim. The pilgrim engages society through any and all of the five social games (see fig. 2.1). The pilgrim has a grasp of the knowledge of the world, understands its economic systems, and is able to use them effectively. While pilgrims grant loyalty to their spiritual house and live in obedience to God, the primary value of engagement with the wider culture is submission for the sake of the gospel and the glory of God. The pilgrim life in the world is driven by the metaphors of the gospel. The metaphors of life and of ministry shape the pilgrim's passage in every social and economic context (Bennett 1993).

The first and most powerful metaphor for the Christian is the cross. Jesus said, "If anyone would come after me, he must deny himself and take up his cross daily and follow me" (Luke 9:23). The metaphor of the cross signifies that the pilgrim lays down her life to find it in Jesus Christ. The pilgrim questions the knowledge of the world, resists the pursuit of significance gained in its social games, and adopts an economic lifestyle oriented toward serving the church and the Lord Jesus Christ.

The second metaphor is that of the servant. Throughout the Gospels Jesus instructed his disciples how to live as servants, awaiting the return of their master. He taught by the power of metaphor in parable, story, and example; his basic command was "Follow me!" The stories of the rich fool, the shrewd manager, the rich man and Lazarus, and the unjust judge depict the way of the world; the stories of the good Samaritan, Mary and Martha, the wise manager, and the father who forgives the prodigal son portray the character and commitments of disciples and servants in the kingdom of God. Luke concludes his record of Jesus' teaching with the story of the dispute among the disciples as to who among them would be the greatest, in which Jesus rebuked them and said, "I am among you as one who serves" (Luke 22:28).

The writers of the Gospels and the epistles record many other metaphors employed by Jesus and the apostles to teach believers how to live as the people of God. "I am the vine; you are the branches. If a man remains in me and I in him, he will bear much fruit; apart from me you can do nothing" (John 15:5). To be a disciple of Jesus is to identify with his compassion and his suffering, to be motivated by his love and caring, to be moved with anger at sin and oppression, and to give one's life for others. Believers are messengers, ambassadors, runners, soldiers, partners, teachers, and shepherds. The power of metaphors lies in their application by analogy to any cultural system or social game. The pilgrim is a player in the social games of culture, but his goals are defined in the cross, and his performance is guided by metaphors from the master.

Which Social Games Do You Play?

It is important to understand yourself before you begin to examine the social games and relationships of others. In the chapters that follow we will explore conflicts over economic and social issues that occur between missionaries and nationals in cross-cultural ministry. We will use the prototype game analysis to demonstrate the root of value conflicts and contradictory assumptions that make it difficult, even impossible, for people to work together. Once you have an understanding of your social values and the social games that you prefer, you will be able to identify the social roots of situations of conflict and tension and apply Scripture in an appropriate way to help you and others live transformed lives.

If you live in a complex industrial society, you probably play a variant of more than one social game. Even in traditional agricultural societies we find clear evidence that people participate in at least two of the prototype social games. These games are not played at the same time but rather organize alternative activities at different space and time. It is typical that people participate in more than one social game in any social setting.

The most common variants in complex Western societies are in the family, church, and workplace. In America the family game varies between rural and urban settings and between ethnic and denominational groups. It is also unusual for any individual to participate in the same social game in his or her family, church, and workplace. As we have seen in the illustrations, American Protestants may choose among all four of the social games in terms of their church affiliation and interests. Similar variations occur in the family and in the workplace.

In the pages that follow I have prepared three different sets of questions that will allow you to test yourself and determine which of the prototypes is most similar to the values, rules, and structure of your family, your church, and your workplace. The multiple-choice questions are scored from zero to ten (0 to 10). Zero (0) signifies the choice of the hermit—complete autonomy—without either grid or group to provide cooperation or constraint in social life. The number ten (10) signifies that grid or group is so strongly developed that individuals cannot effectively engage in social activity apart from their specification for cooperation or constraint. The intermediate numbers (2–8) provide a continuous scale between these extremes with 5 being the midpoint.

Weak Grid 0 —— 2 —— 4 —— 6 —— 8 —— 10 Strong Grid

You will probably find that several of the choices apply to your situation. Typically you should find two or three that apply to your experience, and they will usually cluster together on the continuum. Once you have completed scoring both the grid and the group variables, you will be able to plot the composite score on the social games graph to determine which of the prototype games is most typical of your social life in each of these settings.

The Social Game of Your Workplace (Grid)

The following questions reflect a continuum from 0 to 10. You will find that several answers apply to your workplace. Please *circle the one number* on the continuum for each set of questions that accurately captures the highest expression of grid as practiced in your workplace. If for some reason you find one variable impossible to answer, omit it and calculate the average on the basis of the variables that you have been able to answer effectively.

Weak Grid   0 —— 2 —— 4 —— 6 —— 8 —— 10   **Strong Grid**

1. Is work organized by skill, allowing people to change jobs as the tasks change? and/or 0– No specialists; people choose tasks 2– Job leader; people choose tasks 4– Skilled workers are task leaders	Is work organized in terms of a clearly defined job title, description, and work rules? 6– Some specialist roles; negotiable rules 8– Most roles specialized; flexible rules 10–Strict job specialization, roles, rules
2. Is the work routine variable in response to weather and worker interests? and/or 0– Schedule completely negotiable 2– Schedule around weather constraints 4– Schedule around social events, interests	Is the routine of work established by calendar and daily schedule? 6– Explicit social standards for work routine 8– Public calendar, daily schedule 10– Legal calendar, inflexible schedule
3. Does the boss measure productivity in terms of your effort and goals achieved? and/or 0– Productivity situationally defined 2– Gauged against project goal 4– Gauged against goal, labor expended	Is productivity linked to time limits or product quotas? How are these limits measured? 6– Measure social, economic cost/reward 8– Measure time, labor cost, product goals 10– Precise measures of time and labor costs and production goals and pay-off

4. Is the worker motivated by interest, self-direction, or basic subsistence goals? and/or	By promotion, increased compensation, or threat of punitive action?
0– Labor motivated by self-interest 2– Mutual interests motivate cooperation 4– Skill competition spurs labor effort	6– Promotion competition spurs labor effort 8– Rank and career incentives employed 10– Rank, career, and recognition are primary
5. Are expected outcomes of labor defined and directed by those who do the work? and/or	Do authorities and people who do not work set objectives for those who do?
0– Self-defined objectives 2– Laborers/leader define goals, work pace 4– Workers employ standards of skill, task	6– Leaders consult labor re: goals, process 8– Boss, foremen set goals, direct labor 10– Management defines total labor agenda

The Social Game of Your Workplace (Group)

The following questions reflect a continuum from 0 to 10. You will find that several answers apply to your workplace. Please *circle the one number* on the continuum for each set of questions that accurately captures the highest expression of group as practiced in your workplace.

Weak Group 0 —— 2 —— 4 — 6 —— 8 —— 10 Strong Group

6. Are planning and assignments for workers done by persons initiating/supervising? and/or	Are planning and assignments done by a majority or consensus of the work team?
0– Individually initiated, assigned 2– Individual plans, consults with friends 4– Supervisor, contracted work partners	6– Supervisor/team planning and assignments 8– Majority planning and assignments 10– Team-ruled plan, assignments, sanctions

7. Is cooperative work focused primarily for the profit of cooperating parties? and/or 0– Cooperation strictly self-interest 2– Repeated contracts of cooperating parties 4– Long-term multiple partnerships formed	Focused around shared tradition, interests, and majority or consensus leadership? 6– Majority/leader coordination of projects 8– Consensus leadership of communal work 10– Tradition of collective labor and process
8. Is social interaction excluded, promoting the work activity above social interests? and/or 0– Work excludes social interaction 2– Social interaction only for needed rest 4– Social interaction valued after work	Are relationships between people working as important as the work activity? 6– Work and social interaction blended 8– Social interaction integral to work activity 10– Social goals have priority over economic
9. Is cooperative work "all business" in which people cooperate only as required by the technical demands of the work? and/or 0– Cooperation rare and strictly functional 2– Relationships restricted to workplace 4– Relationships encouraged after work	"Strongly social" with corporate eating, drinking, rituals, and symbolic action as part of the work process? 6– Team building includes family, community 8– Work includes planned social interaction 10– Usual corporate eating, drinking, ritual
10. Are pay-offs private, individual, and according to terms of contract? and/or 0– Personal wages or profit, no celebration 2– Reciprocal labor, meal for workers 4– Personal wages, bonus, and recognition for exceptional achievement	Are pay-offs collective, rewarding success of the group, distributing shares publicly? 6– Wages and profit sharing among members 8– Collective earnings, public distribution 10– Labor a duty of membership, rewarded by celebration, occasional distributions

The Social Game of Your Household (Grid)

Choose either the household in which you grew up or your current household at a time you would consider fairly typical. The following questions reflect a continuum from 0 to 10. You will find that several answers apply to your household and family. Please *circle the one number* on the continuum for each set of questions that accurately captures the highest expression of grid as practiced in your household and family.

Weak Grid 0 —— 2 —— 4 —— 6 —— 8 —— 10 Strong Grid

1. Do parents encourage children to participate in household decisions? and/or 0– Parents provide no direction 2– Parents engage children in family affairs 4– Parents coach children re: expectations	Do parents set boundaries, define duties, and demand obedience? 6– Parents set clear boundaries, roles 8– Parents define duties, responsibilities 10– Parents demand obedience, conformity
2. Are children encouraged to work along side of adults as co-laborers? and/or 0– Children are free of adult responsibility 2– Children accompany parents in routines 4– Children work side by side with adults	Are children's roles structured so as to define specific responsibilities and duties? 6– Children have assigned duties, roles 8– Children's roles structured by age/sex 10– Children serve at the bidding of adults
3. Are age and sex differences of siblings important for domestic duties? and/or 0– Age/sex distinctions insignificant 2– Siblings follow interests, giftedness 4– Older responsible to assist younger	Do elder siblings have authority over younger for economic and social activities? 6– Elder/younger distinction emphasized 8– Elder directs economic, social activity 10– Elder inherits, exercises family authority

4. Do family members perform roles according to their interests? and/or 0– Domestic duties negotiated by parties 2– People exchange tasks, roles over time 4– Roles tend to be stable but not rigid	Are persons restricted to defined roles regardless of personal abilities or interests? 6– Male/female duties are sharply defined 8– All members have prescribed roles 10– Deviation from roles is not tolerated
5. Do parents correct by reference to how pleased, hurt, angry, or disappointed they are by the child's behavior? and/or 0– Parents rarely correct children 2– Parents speak of their pain at child's act 4– Parents show how child's behavior causes pain or pleasure in others	Do parents correct children by reference to social rules and relationships? 6– Parents define roles, rules for behavior 8– Parents correct deviance from roles, rules 10– Children internalize roles, rules, performance expectations

The Social Game of Your Household (Group)

The following questions reflect a continuum from 0 to 10. You will find that several answers apply to your household and family. Please *circle the one number* on the continuum for each set of questions that accurately captures the highest expression of group as practiced in your household and family.

Weak Group 0 —— 2 —— 4 —— 6 —— 8 —— 10 Strong Group

6. Did your household include parents and children? and/or 0– Single-person household 2– Husband/wife independent households 4– Unmarried adult children stay in household	Did it include married children, grandparents, or grandchildren over a 5–10-year period? 6– Newly married couple stay with parents 8– Three generations in household 10– Four generations in household

7. Do husband and wife have responsibility for economic and social decisions? and/or

0– Persons make decisions independently
2– Husband/wife jointly make domestic decisions
4– Husband/wife consult with resident children

Do parents and children together make economic and social decisions?

6– Parent/child consultation expected
8– Parents/adult children jointly decide
10– Corporate sibling decisions are common

---

8. Are members expected to meet their economic needs independently of other kin? and/or

0– Individual controls income, labor
2– Husband/wife pool income, capital
4– Parents/children share capital needs

Does family call upon members periodically to share capital or income or to perform collective labor?

6– Parents/children pool income, capital
8– Extended family shares for capital needs
10– Extended family pools labor, income

---

9. Is residence at marriage a matter of personal choice? and/or

0– Individuals live at distance from both parents
2– Couples live at distance from both parents
4– Couples choose to live near parents

Is residence prescribed by customary practice or rules in the family?

6– Couples live for a time with parents
8– Permanent residence prescribed by group
10– Couples live among and support family group

---

10. Are marriages contracted by the couple and planned in accord with their wishes? and/or

0– elopement (couple run away and marry)
2– families celebrate marriage, departure of couple
4– families give gifts to assist couple begin

Are marriages planned by the families involved?

6– parents approve, help plan marriage
8– bridewealth, dowry essential to marriage
10– marriage arranged by parents of couple

The Social Game of Your Church (Grid)

The following questions reflect a continuum from 0 to 10. You will find that several answers apply to your local church. Please *circle the one number* on the continuum for each set of questions that accurately captures the highest expression of grid as practiced in your local church.

Weak Grid   0 —— 2 —— 4 —— 6 —— 8 —— 10   Strong Grid

1. Does the church recognize the priesthood and ministry of all believers? and/or 0– Each believer may be Spirit-filled 2– Some have gifts of leadership 4– People grant authority to ministry leaders	Does the church recognize professional preparation and a leadership hierarchy? 6– Pastor has a professional role 8– Elders, pastoral staff in hierarchy of roles 10– Hierarchy of ordained clergy oversees church ministries
2. Do people engage in bargaining and dialogue to reach collective decisions? and/or 0– Individuals make personal decisions 2– People collaborate from shared interests 4– An influential few negotiate for many	Are a few people empowered to make decisions for others? 6– Elected pastor plays key role in decisions 8– Decisions by church board, staff 10– Decisions by clergy and staff
3. Does the leader's power rest in people who personally grant or deny support? and/or 0– Individuals refuse to support leaders 2– Individuals grant support to worthy leaders 4– Leaders build a network of influence	Is power delegated by a board or a staff to subordinates, and in what specific ways? 6– Pastor delegates to lay ministry team 8– Church board delegates power to staff 10– Bishop, clergy hold and delegate power

4. Is support for ministry (labor, finances) raised by the individuals involved? and/or 0– Individuals finance their own ministries 2– Each ministry raises support 4– Leaders coordinate and inspire support for ministries	Is control over labor, finances, and resources held by the pastor or governing board? 6– Majority control budget and staff 8– Board controls budget and staff 10– Bishop, clergy control budget and staff
5. In return for support do people expect pastoral ministry of worship, healing, and power? and/or 0– God rewards those who seek him 2– Church a community of worship, healing 4– Leaders minister through Scripture and spiritual power	Do they expect pastoral ministry of baptism, doctrine, communion, confession, and mission? 6– Pastors are experts on doctrine, practice 8– Pastors/elders govern in doctrine, practice 10– Bishops and clergy administer the sacraments of the church

The Social Game of Your Church (Group)

The following questions reflect a continuum from 0 to 10. You will find that several answers apply to your local church. Please *circle the one number* on the continuum for each set of questions that accurately captures the highest expression of group as practiced in your local church.

Weak Group 0 —— 2 —— 4 —— 6 —— 8 —— 10 Strong Group

6. Are individual words of prophecy and biblical interpretation valued? and/or 0– God may give prophetic vision to each 2– Individual walk with God highly valued 4– Bible-centered, varying interpretation	Do members emphasize a common heritage of faith and doctrine and exclude dissidents? 6– Core beliefs shared with variance in detail 8– Authoritative system of belief, faith 10– Uniform doctrine, exclusion of dissidents

7. Do people build relationships upon mutual ministry commitments? and/or 0– Church open, no membership 2– People identify primarily as "attenders" 4– People commit to ministry groups	Do people build relationships upon church symbols, membership, and practice? 6– Ministry leadership by members only 8– Church standards, ordinances mark membership 10– Mature elders serve in place of formal pastors
8. Do individuals or interest groups impose decisions in spite of opposition of others? and/or 0– Personal power overrides process 2– Participants maneuver to gain advantage 4– Influence directs decision process	Are decisions for the church controlled by a majority at least and by consensus at best? 6– Decisions by majority with minority voice 8– Discussion ongoing until members agree 10– Decisions by consensus, binding on all
9. Is individual support to leaders conditional upon meeting personal interests? and/or 0– People support leaders they admire 2– Leaders negotiate, compromise for support 4– People are loyal to leaders who help them	Is support for leaders expected because of membership loyalty? 6– People are loyal first to the church 8– People are loyal, even as a minority voice 10– Loyalty is more important than interests or leadership
10. Do attenders come to meet spiritual needs and achieve personal ministry? and/or 0– Attending meets personal needs, goals 2– People do ministries of personal interest 4– Belonging and ministry persist even in times of disappointment and distress	Do members value long-term loyalty and commitment to the group and its values? 6– Membership confers valued relationships 8– Members become family and community 10– Members sacrifice personal interests for church commitments and service

Sample*	Workplace	Household	Church
GRID SCORES:	GRID SCORES:	GRID SCORES:	GRID SCORES:
1. _4_	1. _____	1. _____	1. _____
2. _2_	2. _____	2. _____	2. _____
3. _4_	3. _____	3. _____	3. _____
4. _4_	4. _____	4. _____	4. _____
5. _2_	5. _____	5. _____	5. _____
Sum: _16_	Sum: _____	Sum: _____	Sum: _____
GROUP SCORES:	GROUP SCORES:	GROUP SCORES:	GROUP SCORES:
6. _8_	6. _____	6. _____	6. _____
7. _6_	7. _____	7. _____	7. _____
8. _8_	8. _____	8. _____	8. _____
9. _6_	9. _____	9. _____	9. _____
10. _8_	10. _____	10. _____	10. _____
Sum: _36_	Sum: _____	Sum: _____	Sum: _____
AVERAGES	AVERAGES	AVERAGES	AVERAGES
Grid: _(3.2)_	Grid: _____	Grid: _____	Grid: _____
Group: _(7.2)_	Group: _____	Group: _____	Group: _____

Once you have completed calculating the grid and group averages for each situation, please plot the exact position (*S for the sample) of your workplace, household, and church on the graph (p. 50). The graph will show you which social game you play in each of these areas of your life and how strongly or weakly your situation matches the ideal prototype games.

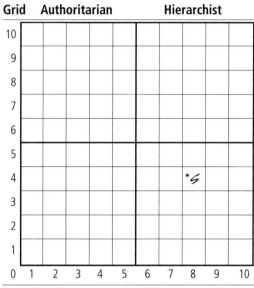

3
Property
The Silent Enemy of Church Growth

A pastor of a successful English/Spanish inner-city church in Los Angeles often receives invitations to challenge people in his denomination to reach out to Hispanics and other ethnic groups in southern California, yet he finds people less than eager to follow his lead. On one occasion, when he pointed out the responsibility of suburban Christians to minister to the poor and foreigners, a parishioner interrupted with evident irritation. Pointing to the steeple on top of the church, he said, "See that steeple up there? I built it with my own hands. No Mexican is ever going to be on the board of this church as long as I have anything to do with it!"

This parishioner is hardly unique. Many evangelicals, from the mission field to the local church, share his frustrations, concerns, and prejudices. Investment in property and values about property stir deep emotions among American Christians.

Case Studies

A Fruit Tree in California

The anxiety among Anglo Christians about personal or church property is one of the key obstacles to reaching immigrant populations in southern California. After a Sunday service in which I spoke on this subject, a member of the congregation shared the following story. A few years before, Vietnamese children came to his house and asked if they could pick the fruit from a tree in his yard. He allowed them to do so. In their enthusiasm they broke numerous small branches. Distressed at the appearance of the tree after they had finished, he decided that he would not let them pick fruit again. Over the next couple of years, when the fruit was ripe, the children pestered him to pick fruit, but each time he turned them away. Even though the fruit fell to the ground and rotted, he did not want to deal with the trouble or the damage these children might cause. Finally, in frustration over their continual asking, he cut down the tree.

As this man told me the story, he was aware of the lost opportunity to share the love of Christ with many children who had come to his house for fruit. The tree had become the focus of his interest. Compelled to protect his interest, he cut the tree down rather than share its fruit with those who had need. Not only did he fail to share his abundance, but also he failed to share the good news of Christ with those who came. His situation is not unique. Many people have chosen to protect property rather than to share the good news of Christ. He said, "I have been so blind. The Lord has been bringing people to my door, but instead of reaching out, I have turned them away and cut down the tree that brought them. To protect my property and privacy, I have lost a great opportunity." Missionaries schooled in the same social game experience similar frustrations on the mission field.

Property Maintenance in Central Africa

A pastor friend in southern California related the story of a visit to his denominational mission in Africa. At one mission station, a missionary complained bitterly to him about the time he had to spend on maintenance at the station. He said, "I spend 90 percent of my time on maintenance and only 10 percent on ministry. I am deeply frustrated! Please carry the message back to our churches of how desperately we need maintenance help."

The missionary described how disputes about property had alienated him from his African neighbors. Complaining that they had no respect for private property, he described how hostile neighbors frequently cut the plastic water pipe that brought water from his storage tank. Sometimes a woman was "too lazy" to walk to the river for water and used the convenient method of cutting his pipe to supply her need. Needless to say, he responded angrily to these acts of vandalism, which also created a hardship for the missionaries by draining their water supply.

Neither the pastor nor the missionary considered the possibility of forgetting the maintenance and getting on with the ministry. The maintenance of the property was of higher priority than the ministry of the gospel in that missionary's life. He would not say this with his words, but he clearly showed it by his actions.

The missionary maintained the property because he was compelled to do so by his and the mission's social values and resultant expectations. Having learned from the time he was a boy that property has great value and must be preserved and sustained, he and his colleagues believed that to fail to do so was sin. He felt a moral responsibility to keep up the property, even though that responsibility kept him from ministering to the people for whom he had gone to the mission field.

Property and Ministry

Stories like the ones already related can be retold on every continent of the world. Missionaries open up new fields and plant churches. Inevitably, after the harvesting of souls they find it necessary to build a church building. Oftentimes they deem local materials inadequate, because if one is to build a building one should do it right ("right" usually means the way it was done at home). The missionary may solicit money from home churches to build an impressive building, evidence of God's power and wondrous work in this place. The dedication of the new church is frequently followed by other building projects. Sometimes it is a school, sometimes a youth center, sometimes a bookstore, sometimes housing for other missionaries. Often these building projects take years of work and energy, with negative impacts on evangelism and church planting. The growth of the church becomes internal, through the children of converts. Evangelism dies out, and the ministry now becomes one of nurturing the flock.

Missionaries have many responsibilities in maintaining physical facilities. Buildings must be painted. It is not good to have a building without grass, but grass must be mowed. Of course it is important to have motor vehicles to save travel time with so many responsibilities, but cars require maintenance and upkeep. And as the missionary compound grows so does the work to keep it running, and field workers find themselves in the situation of the missionary in Africa, spending 90 percent of their time on maintenance and only 10 percent on ministry.

Many mission organizations try to rectify this situation by sending more missionaries to the field. Only a few of these new missionaries are involved in evangelism and church planting. Most come in supporting roles, to maintain the property, to teach in the schools, to work in the print shop, to supervise the youth center, and to keep running the system set up by the first wave of church planters. All of this new staff serve at great expense to the home church and in the long run contribute more of their energy and work to the property than to the ministry of the mission. Church growth slows when the building program begins, and it rarely regains its momentum.

Only by increasing the missionary staff threefold can a mission effect a sustained program of evangelism and discipleship. In many of the missions conferences I attend, I find mission leaders appealing for support workers to do the jobs that will free the evangelists and teachers for evangelism and teaching. I hear very few people asking if some or many of these jobs could be eliminated or how to mobilize evangelists and teachers with minimal property and equipment.

What values compel us to commit ourselves so inextricably to property, whether in our ministries at home or abroad? Why are buildings so important for a dynamic, growing ministry? Why do we fight so strongly to protect and preserve our property? How is it that we allow concern for material possessions to come between us and our call to ministry? What can we do to focus clearly on these conflicts and to identify alternative strategies to cope with them? How can we begin to make choices that enable us to be more effective in our relationships and ministry?

Property and Social Values

How do the social games we adopt for ministry shape our values for property? How do weak and strong grid generate different values regarding property, and what variations do we see in cultures? What is the ongoing tension between the individual and the group in relationship to property? How do strong group social games create value conflicts for missionaries and pastors from weak group games?

Grid: Holding versus Competition for Property

Let us first consider the issue of grid. How is the individual's personal estate significant in terms of conception of self, personal significance, and uniqueness? If people have no personal estate (the hermit)—in other words, no property of significance—then property constitutes little or no risk and contributes little to conception of self in society. When property ownership is important to individuals, then property confers significant social and economic value and risk to those who hold it. It becomes important in a person's conception of self and social esteem.

In the authoritarian and hierarchist social games (strong grid) control over property is usually connected to those who hold the higher positions in the social hierarchy, and people place high priority on holding property. Since property often confers personal prestige and symbolizes social class, preservation of holdings becomes a high value. People learn to conserve their resources and thereby enhance their social standing. Achievement in this setting is highly structured by factors of status and role to which property values have been attached. Saving becomes a high value, and individuals are motivated to protect their personal property interests (fig. 3.1).

In individualist and egalitarian social games (weak grid) competition rather than control is the primary value. The increased individual autonomy of low grid dictates freedom to manage property according to individual designs. Where property confers economic advantage or power, individuals may engage in significant risk taking to expand their property holdings and thereby improve their personal position and reputation. Achievement in this environment is associated with risk and investment of individual energy and skill. The individualist game promotes a free-for-all attitude toward acquiring and risking property. The egalitarian game quenches too much entrepreneurship by its demands that people share their good fortune with others in the group.

Group: Individual Interests versus Corporate Interests

Group control over property is an ancient practice in human societies. When Joshua divided the land of Canaan among the tribes of Israel, he distributed the territories according to groups—the tribes, clans, and families of Israel. Careful examination of the historical books in the Old Testament shows that rights to land in Israel were held by both the individual and the group. The law stated clearly that land could not be alienated from the group. If for some reason people were forced to sell their land, during the sabbatical (seventh) year or in the year of jubilee all alienated lands were to be returned to those families from which they had been separated.

This corporate principle is illustrated further in the Book of Ruth. Naomi was not free to sell her lands to anyone she pleased but had to follow the required rules of succession that granted rights to those lands to other members of her husband's clan and lineage. Boaz, according to the text, was not the first in line to inherit the property, and so he had to negotiate settlement with the kinsman who had first priority. It became clear as they negotiated for the property (Ruth 4) that it was not merely property at stake but also a person. Naomi's kinsman not only had to redeem the property but also had to marry Ruth and provide for her descendants. For this reason the kinsman redeemer gave up his rights to Boaz.

This tension between individual and group rights is an important issue in understanding property cross-culturally. Some societies place a strong emphasis on individual control, whereas others focus on corporate control.

In the individualist and authoritarian (low group) social games participants spurn collective considerations, having only instrumental or material interest in cooperation. Acquiring, rather than sharing, motivates individual behavior, and the use and consumption of property are governed by individual considerations. Self-interest has priority over other persons, shaping economic and social decisions.

Figure 3.1
Social Games and Property Priorities

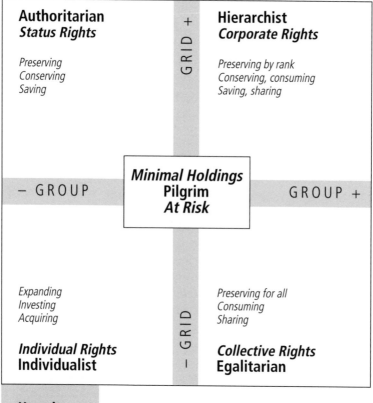

Authoritarian
Status Rights

Preserving
Conserving
Saving

GRID +

Hierarchist
Corporate Rights

Preserving by rank
Conserving, consuming
Saving, sharing

– GROUP

Minimal Holdings
Pilgrim
At Risk

GROUP +

Expanding
Investing
Acquiring

GRID –

Preserving for all
Consuming
Sharing

Individual Rights
Individualist

Collective Rights
Egalitarian

Hermit

In hierarchist and egalitarian (high group) social games the priority of persons and group interests dominate social values. Members of groups place strong value upon sharing with one another and to a lesser degree with outsiders. Leaders may demand that members contribute family or personal property for the interest of the group, and they will sanction those individuals who fail to contribute. The group will mobilize to protect its collective property against the threat of outsiders and to redistribute its resources fairly among its members.

Property Values and Ministry Conflicts

Returning to the case studies at the beginning of the chapter, we can now see that the layman with the fruit tree and the missionary shared similar values. Each was preoccupied with the preservation of property; each placed great emphasis on maintaining the existing value of the property; and each was defensive about outsiders who threatened his property interests. These values are typical of the authoritarian and hierarchist social games. The layman who built the church steeple was perhaps motivated by egalitarian values; the church was his investment, and no outsider had a right to a place on the board of owners.

In each case, conflict arose because of interaction with others who represented different identities and social games. The suburban church member viewed Mexican neighbors as a threat to a building that he had helped construct. The Anglo neighbor was distressed at how the Vietnamese children damaged his tree in picking its fruit. The American missionary in Central Africa felt harassed by his African neighbors who insisted on obtaining unauthorized access to his water by cutting the plastic pipe.

While we do not have adequate data to determine what precise social game these "outsiders" played, it is evident from their behavior that they valued sharing. The African woman cut the water line because she needed water and the missionary refused to share a valued water source. The Vietnamese children asked to pick fruit because they saw it falling to the ground and rotting. The inner-city pastor asked the suburban church member to share his facilities with Hispanic immigrants living in the neighborhood.

In each case, those involved responded with deep emotion. They were not able to think objectively about the situation or make a decision based upon the real needs of the people involved. They responded from deep feelings and emotional values rooted in a particular worldview.

The effect of every social game is to squeeze its members into a particular social and value mold. The African who cuts the water line is acting from social values, as is the missionary who is angered by the act. Both of them are products of their social contexts and worldviews, albeit different ones. Neither is able to actualize the admonition of Romans 12:2 *(Phillips)*: "Do not allow the world to squeeze you into its mold."

In all three situations, the values expressed by these Christians are in conflict with their Christian faith. The Synoptic Gospels are replete with metaphors for how priority for property should be peripheral in the life of the Christian disciple. Matthew 6:19–24 calls the believer to lay up treasures in heaven rather than on earth. In the same chapter (vv. 28–34) Jesus challenges his disciples to "consider the lilies of the field" (KJV), not to worry about clothing or food "but [to] seek first his kingdom and his righteousness, and all these things will be given to you as well." Matthew 19:16–22 recounts the story of the rich young man who came to Jesus and asked what good thing he needed to do to gain eternal life. Jesus told him to sell his possessions and give to the poor. The young man went away in despair, because he had great wealth.

In spite of these texts, missionaries struggle more with nationals over property than perhaps in any other area of their relationships. Some missionary candidates have asked us if it is acceptable to take a microwave oven and an ample supply of shoes and clothing for their children. Their rationale is that things are cheaper in the United States than in the country to which they are going. When they arrive in their field of ministry and find people asking them for the things they have brought, they must defend and protect their property interests. All of this results in spiritual as well as social struggle. Pacific Island missionaries have engaged in endless disputes with national leaders over the use of mission vehicles. Missionaries living in compounds in Brazil and Africa struggle with pressure to dissolve their compounds and enter the national society and culture. In all of these situations nationals view missionaries as both wealthy and stingy, denying the benefits of their wealth to national co-workers.

These missionaries know the text in Mark 6:8–11 in which Jesus instructs his disciples to go with no bread, no bag, no money, and no extra clothing. They find such instructions incomprehensible and archaic, clearly not applicable to their life and ministry. They have read many times Luke 9:58: "foxes have holes, and birds of the air have nests, but the Son of Man has no place to lay his head." They know of the cost of discipleship described in Matthew 16:24–28 and Luke 14:33: "any of you who does not give up everything he has cannot be my disciple." Some may even recall Hebrews 10:32–34, which talks about how early believers joyfully accepted the confiscation of their property. Yet the pull of their own social game is so powerful that they can only with extreme difficulty incorporate such principles into their own lives and relationships.

Students and missionary candidates are no different from their predecessors in the field. Some of the most common questions I am asked in my classes have to do with anticipated requests for money and personal property. Usually these students are concerned about someone taking advantage of them, about not having enough for themselves, and about stewardship and using wisely the resources they have been given.

I should make it clear that neither I nor the Scriptures are antiwealth or antireward. Luke 19:11–27 relates the parable of the ten minas, in which the faithful servants are given great reward for their faithful service. It is clear in Luke 8:2–3 that women of means supported Jesus and his disciples in their itinerant ministry. Jesus loved and accepted those who had wealth, and he owed his personal support in large part to these women of means. Jesus' disciples were also property owners. Peter, James, and John came from families that owned houses and fishing boats. They were independent businessmen who supported their families through the property resources that they held. Barnabas perhaps paid the bills on his trips with Paul; Paul had a room in Philemon's house and requested the service of one of his slaves.

The issue is not having wealth or property but rather the values that lie behind our attitudes toward property and ministry. Acts 4:37 notes how one of the disciples, Barnabas, sold a field that he owned and brought the money to the apostles. The text does not say that he sold all of his property, but only a field. It also records how he did this to encourage and support those who had need.

As we reflect on the four distinctive social games and their respective values, it should be clear that each frames specific values in relationship to property. A careful examination of each of the social games may produce critical insight into ways in which these values are used with respect to other people. The biblical metaphors suggest that we seek freedom from the bondage of property regardless of the social game in which we find ourselves. The rich young ruler described in the three Gospels probably reflected hierarchist social values in his family and workplace. As is true of the Christian workers in our stories, property was a stumbling block, interfering with his relationship with Jesus Christ. He was unable to accept a call to ministry because he valued his property more highly than eternal life.

Christian Pilgrimage and Property

To work toward the resolution of conflicts about property, we must first identify our fears. When holding property is important, then losing it becomes more important. The question of risk lies at the root of our fears. Fear is always a significant obstacle to a life of Christian pilgrimage. Once we identify our fears, we may then deal with them through application of the truth of Scripture.

The man who owned the fruit tree was upset by its appearance, perhaps fearing that it was a negative reflection on him. Each subsequent year when the fruit was ripe he was further frustrated by the loss of peace and quiet and the inconvenience created by children coming to his door. The fear of disruption of his personal life finally led him to cut the tree down. As this man reflected on his actions, he identified two key principles that are crucial for Christian workers. The tree created an opportunity for building relationships with people he did not know. Each child asking for fruit from his tree presented another opportunity to share the love of Christ. If we can interpret requests for access to our property as an opportunity to demonstrate our love in Christ, our attitude about the person making the request and the potential depletion of our resources will change drastically. Fear of inconvenience and fear of loss of image pale in contrast to the opportunity to build relationships and to proclaim Christ.

If we could ask the missionary in Central Africa what fears pushed him to spend 90 percent of his time on maintenance, he might include fear of an inadequate water supply; fear of breakdown of necessary equipment; fear of the loss of time because of the failure to do preventive maintenance; discouragement over the disorder in his living circumstances; and fear of being dependent upon others who might be helpful but only with strings attached. Property begins to own the missionary instead of the missionary owning the property. Preservation becomes a matter of preserving self-identity and well-being, as well as fending off disorder.

Jesus admonishes us to not fear for these things. He calls us to a life of pilgrimage, playing any or all of the social games yet minimizing our holdings and living at risk (fig. 3.1). Yet our faith is often weak, and we cry out for a few practical strategies. The most important strategy is to adopt a simplified lifestyle. The less property we own, the less energy we will have to expend to prevent disorder. By simplifying their lifestyle Christian workers remove the temptation to hang on to the social values of their home culture.

Missionaries must also relinquish independence and become more dependent (at risk) on nationals. In Central Africa, for example, many women would be happy to earn money by carrying water for missionaries. While the men would need to learn to do maintenance work, they would be delighted to have jobs. If missionaries learn to accept less precision and be open to alternative ways of accomplishing things, they will probably find that national workers can take care of most of the maintenance that must be done. Further, the mutual relationship between missionary and national worker can become a means of discipling new believers.

To help us change our attitudes we may challenge one another with the question, Whom do we worship: God or the creation of our hands? Reviewing Scripture passages such as Isaiah 44 can help us come to terms with the issue of false worship. Only when we are willing to surrender to Christ all that we have are we free to enjoy all that he gives to us. Jesus reminds us in the Gospels that if we struggle to save our lives we are certain to lose them.

The solution for the Christian worker, then, is to not be enslaved to the values of his or her social game. Norman Dietsch, a missionary to people on the island of Manus in New Guinea, told me the story of how he was instructed by his colleagues to buy pots and pans, plates, utensils, towels, and other items to set up his household as a single man in Manus. When he arrived on the beach, the Manus people (egalitarian) began to request from him each of the items that he had obediently purchased. As Dietsch tells his story, he said he naively accepted the text in Matthew 5:42 that says "give to the one who asks you, and do not turn away from the one who wants to borrow from you." Soon, all of the items that he had purchased were gone; the people had taken every one. But then Dietsch discovered a marvelous thing. When he needed to cook, all he had to do was ask, and there was always a pan available. When he needed utensils, they were provided. When he needed a towel, someone always produced a towel. During that first year of ministry the people were faithful to their own value for sharing, providing every one of his material needs, returning in kind everything that he had given to them.

The point of this illustration is that living a life of pilgrimage does not place the Christian at risk, in spite of the fact that our background values cry out against the action path demanded. God is faithful to his people and rewards those who obey his commandments. The challenge for Christian workers is to learn to discern when the values of their social game become obstacles to obedience.

4
Labor and Productivity
Divisive Values in Mission

Case Studies

The Deni and Mission Conflict

The Deni, located on Marrecao Creek in the Cunhua/Purus river region in western Brazil, were studied by Gordon Koop in the mid-1970s. Koop was residing among them to translate the New Testament into their language. I joined him as an anthropology consultant in 1977 and spent several months conducting research with him in the village (Koop and Lingenfelter 1980). The Deni are farmers, hunters, and fishermen. This particular Deni village, situated in clearings in a vast tropical jungle, had only sixteen households of eighty-six people. The adaptation of these people to the hardships and hostilities of life in the Amazon rain forest, with only peripheral contact with Brazilians, provides an example of how aboriginal people play individualist and egalitarian social games to survive.

In his work with these people Koop occasionally sent radio messages to Deni villagers asking them to clear the airstrip of grass and jungle weeds in preparation for his return to the village. Understanding the importance of the task and the urgency

to have it completed before the day of the scheduled flight, the
people responded promptly; they generally cleared and maintained the airstrip to the satisfaction of the pilot.

Koop's problem came in paying the people for their work. Most
of the villagers had worked on the strip, and they all expected
some pay for their work. Because he was not in the village, Koop
found it impossible to distinguish between those who worked
hard and long and those who had merely come to collect a
reward. He wanted to pay people according to the quality and
time of their work, and he wanted each person to be treated fairly.
He also had limited funds and could not give indiscriminately.

Asking the village chief to pay people according to the amount
of work that they had done, Koop provided a quantity of shotgun powder and enough bolts of cloth to pay men and women
what he deemed an appropriate fee for the work. The village
chief took the shotgun powder and the cloth to his house and
invited the men and women who had worked to come. The
aggressive men quickly took as much powder as they could get,
and the aggressive women took more than their share of cloth,
leaving those who were less aggressive with little or nothing.

The disgruntled workers complained to Koop, who was deeply
frustrated by the whole process. He confronted the chief, telling
him of those who were angry and reprimanding him for not paying people according to their work. The chief in turn told Koop
that there was not enough material to satisfy all the people who
had worked. Koop tried to explain that he had given enough,
but the chief did not distribute it properly. The outcome was a
stand-off: Koop said the chief was weak and let things get out
of control; the chief and people said Koop had the goods, but he
would not give enough to pay everybody. All grumbled openly
about the others who had grabbed for themselves.

Nehemiah and the Wall

The Book of Nehemiah in the Old Testament provides a very
different case study of the organization of labor. Nehemiah came
from the citadel of Susa to his ancestral home in Jerusalem with
letters from King Artaxerxes authorizing him to cut timber and
to rebuild the city gates and city walls of Jerusalem. After sur-

veying the ruins (Neh. 2:13–16), Nehemiah informed the priests, nobles, and officials that he had received authorization from the king and organized them to begin the work of rebuilding the walls.

Nehemiah used two key principles for the organization of the workforce: residence and kinship. The text (Neh. 3) details how each gate was assigned to a particular leader and the residents of a particular district. In most of these situations the residents of districts were also kinsmen or extended families. Nehemiah assigned repairs on the walls to leaders of particular districts in the region or to families who lived immediately adjacent to a particular section of the wall. It is clear from reading through the text that each gate and each section was repaired by an assigned work group. The work was organized along the lines of existing leadership, territorial, and kinship divisions within the society.

The local governor, Sanballat, opposed the work of Nehemiah, seeing him as a threat to his own leadership and promoting the welfare of the subject Israelite population. He attempted to arouse other ethnic groups in the region to mobilize against the Israelites and stop them, even by force, from completing this task. Nehemiah reports that there was intense opposition and fear of attack among the people working on the project.

Nehemiah responded to this threat by organizing half of his workforce for defense and the other half for labor. "I stationed some of the people behind the lowest points of the wall at the exposed places, posting them by families, with their swords, spears, and bows. After I looked things over, I stood up and said to the nobles, the officials and the rest of the people, 'Don't be afraid of them. Remember the Lord, who is great and awesome, and fight for your brothers, your sons and your daughters, your wives, and your homes'" (Neh. 4:13–14). From that time on, half of the people worked while the other half stood guard against the threat of hostile outside forces. Nehemiah kept a man with a trumpet near him and told the workers and warriors to come to the sound of the trumpet to quell any attack from their enemies.

During this same time, the people apparently had experienced a famine. The poorer members of the community were forced to mortgage their fields, vineyards, and homes to get adequate grain to eat. Nehemiah confronted the nobles and officials, accusing them of exacting interest from their countrymen and forcing them into slavery. He insisted that these wealthy leaders lend money and grain to the people without interest and without confiscating their fields, vineyards, olive groves, and houses (Neh. 5:9–11). Nehemiah reports that he had ample food to feed the 150 Jews and officials who ate at his table, but he did not demand the food allotted to the governor because he felt the tax load on the people was already too heavy.

Working at what seemed an impossible pace, the people labored day and night, completing the rebuilding of the wall in fifty-two days. Nehemiah reports, "Neither I nor my brothers nor my men nor the guards with me took off our clothes; each had his weapon, even when he went for water" (Neh. 4:23). Through his leadership, he inspired the people to finish this great task and thereby remove their disgrace, shame, and vulnerability.

Labor and Social Games

Nehemiah and Koop faced very different social games for the organization of work. Nehemiah found an existing political organization with a hierarchy of leadership and an organization of residential and kinship groups. Playing a hierarchist game, these groups had a history of cooperative labor and were mobilized quickly for a task that seemed impossible to their enemies. They worked intensively and collectively and supported one another for the corporate objective of rebuilding the walls of Jerusalem. Koop, in contrast, faced a group of unorganized, self-motivated, and independent workers. Playing an individualist game, each of them expected payment from him according to their own estimation of their work. They had no effective centralized leadership and were unaccustomed to any kind of corporate work activity or corporate reward (see fig. 4.1).

Labor and productivity may be measured by two key characteristics: the extent to which labor and productivity are organized by rule or goal and the extent to which labor is left to the decision of the individual or is governed by group relationships. The unique emphasis upon one or more of these factors in a social game leads to particular values and practices for social labor. The life and labor of a hermit are wholly self-directed and self-fulfilling. Whether farming a small subsistence plot in a forest, trapping and hunting game in the wilderness, or scavenging in the garbage bins of an urban metropolis, the hermit works alone, in accord with his or her personal needs and interests. Eschewing social relationships, the hermit need only satisfy personal needs and wants.

Figure 4.1
Social Games and Labor Priorities

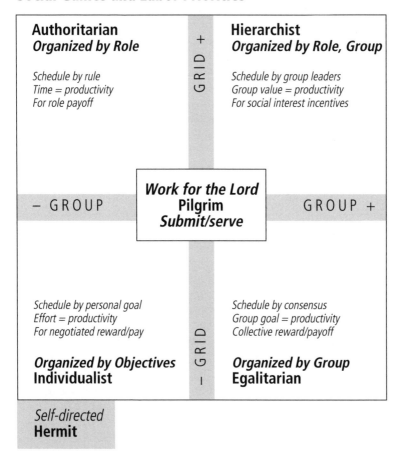

Authoritarian
Organized by Role

Schedule by rule
Time = productivity
For role payoff

GRID +

Hierarchist
Organized by Role, Group

Schedule by group leaders
Group value = productivity
For social interest incentives

− GROUP

Work for the Lord
Pilgrim
Submit/serve

GROUP +

Schedule by personal goal
Effort = productivity
For negotiated reward/pay

Organized by Objectives
Individualist

GRID −

Schedule by consensus
Group goal = productivity
Collective reward/payoff

Organized by Group
Egalitarian

Self-directed
Hermit

In contrast the individualist labor game is social, competitive, and goal-directed. As Koop found with the Deni, workers had clear ideas about what they should be paid and aggressively demanded and seized what they believed was due. Getting more than others did not trouble them, and if one could work less and get more, so be it! Workers who were cheated of their pay made it clear they would not work again and continued to make their discontent known. Koop was at a loss to know how to lead these people.

When Nehemiah returned to Jerusalem with a mission on his mind, he walked into a hierarchist community, already well organized for a corporate labor project. Nehemiah appealed to their corporate sense of honor and responsibility. He organized competing social divisions in the community into productive, motivated labor units. Because of the opposition of outsiders, he was able to motivate people to set other tasks aside and commit to an intense work schedule. The hierarchist game, utilizing social-interest incentives and organization by role and group and measuring productivity in terms of corporate values, made Nehemiah's leadership task much easier than Gordon Koop's.

The most familiar expression of the authoritarian labor game is the modern industrial bureaucracy. Businesses, government agencies, and universities frequently structure their management and labor. These bureaucracies tend to isolate individual workers with sharply defined job descriptions and work rules. They schedule labor and compensation by hourly or salary classification and evaluate employee productivity in relation to time spent on the job. Group motivation, typical of hierarchist and egalitarian social games, is noticeably absent. Koop tried to organize Deni labor around these basic principles.

Egalitarian labor games are collectivist in their organization and compensation. While this structure of labor is less common in Western industrial societies, mission groups sometimes organize around these principles. In one contemporary mission, members work in egalitarian field teams. All members have the same level of financial support. They work together to define team goals, schedule, and personal ministries within the team context. They share collective team resources, pray for needs collectively, and celebrate the accomplishments of the team and its members.

Labor and Ministry Conflicts

Mission Employment of Aukan Co-Workers

The case of the Aukan Bible translation project in Surinam illustrates the tension between authoritarian and egalitarian labor games. The Aukan and Saramaccan people are descendants of slaves brought from Africa to Surinam on the northern coast of South America. Each of these language groups is scattered throughout the interior of Surinam, living on islands and along the banks of the two major rivers and in the capital city of Paramaribo. These villagers, whose ancestors escaped from the slave plantations and reestablished a matrilineally focused culture, practice ancestor veneration and exhibit many other cultural features carried with them from West Africa generations ago. Mission relationships with Aukan and occasionally the Saramaccan people are described in many of the following chapters. While I have visited both groups and worked with mission teams who have long-term and intimate knowledge of each, I am indebted to the work of Louis Shanks (1987) for detailed information on this project.

Bible translators in the city of Paramaribo sought to enlist the support of local churches for the Aukan translation project. Mission staff desired that the local Aukan churches support two individuals they had chosen to be translation workers. These two men were multilingual; they could read and write in Dutch and in English and had been trained to write in their own language and to translate. However, they were relatively young men who were not recognized in the church as spiritual leaders. Mission leaders felt that the churches ought to provide partial support for these men to do translation work and sought to motivate church leaders to support them.

The elders in the churches not only refused to provide economic support for these men but also questioned whether they should be entrusted with the responsibility of translation. When the mission team explored the situation further, they discovered that the pastors did not receive pay. Rather, they were working for the Lord; they were chosen by the senior pastors because of their long-term commitment to and work for the group. They had demonstrated faithfulness over many years in supporting group interests and working toward group goals; as a consequence they were entrusted with the spiritual leadership of the group.

In contrast, the Bible translators were primarily concerned about the technical requirements of the work. They defined Bible translation in bureaucratic management terms (see fig. 4.2). They had a job they wanted done. This job required certain technical skills and individuals who could fill that goal assignment. The mother-tongue translator was a role, and the task was an assignment to be done by rule and paid according to time-work equivalents. The church, in contrast, had no rule of time-work equivalents but rather of work-group equivalents (egalitarian labor teams). Individuals should be working for the group because as members it was in their interest to do so. Their legitimacy was established by the quality and the duration of their work. These young men not only should not be paid but also should be working to demonstrate their spiritual maturity by giving their time and energy to projects of interest to the group.

The Bible translators held to their own work strategies but recognized that they had to provide the pay for these mother-tongue translators. Since the job was defined according to the Bible translators' hierarchy and work rules, it was impractical to expect the Aukan church to support it. The two systems were in distinct conflict with one another, and a resolution would require a change in the social structure of either of the two groups. Neither was willing or able to change.

This kind of social conflict is inevitable as we attempt to move from one social setting to another. The Aukan churches mobilized members for group interests with a high level of effectiveness. On several occasions we observed many Aukan men working together around the church building to maintain it, to clean it, and to make improvements on the general property. They also organized themselves to care for the membership. Different individuals had responsibilities for visiting the sick, for holding Bible studies, or for organizing youth activities. All of these individuals worked for the Lord and for the good of the group. None of them received pay, including the senior pastor. Individuals received leadership responsibility because of their regular, consistent performance in support of the work of the group. The

Figure 4.2
Mission and Aukan Labor Assumptions

Authoritarian *Mission Management*	Hierarchist
Task, skill authority Delegated power Decisions from top Structural support	
	Personal authority Allocated power Consensus decisions Symbolic support *Aukan Management*
Individualist	Egalitarian

success of the group was its own reward, and individuals received only prestige rewards and recognition for their commitment to group goals.

Outside of the church many of these individuals held jobs in the national economy. The pastor whom we interviewed worked for the national government and was paid for his role and work. It is not that these urban Aukan did not understand the other arrangements; many of them worked in bureaucratic labor environments. However, they could not redefine their egalitarian church environment. They saw the Bible translators as an institution like the Surinam government, capable of paying out of its own resources for technical work. As a consequence, the Aukan did not see and could not appreciate why the Bible translators wanted them to support the Bible translation efforts of these two men. As members of the church these men should work in secular jobs as did the other people in the church and support the group and its interests. Bible translation was in the group interest, but it was not a group project; it was the Bible translators' project. Therefore, it was only right that they should pay these men to do Bible translation if they wanted them to do it. The concept of church support for translation was inconsistent with church work procedures and in conflict with the Aukans' understanding of how the church should work.

These Aukan people know and play two different labor games in the same setting. Yet they clearly separate the two and see them as incompatible. Conflicts will arise when we attempt to mix these kinds of social expectations and rules about work and overturn the social structures within which they are contextualized. The labor context of the Bible translators requires work by rule and procedures characteristic of bureaucracy and authoritarian games. The work in the Aukan church requires work by goal, the primacy of group interest, and procedures characteristic of egalitarian games. When the mission leaders demanded that an egalitarian church support a project according to authoritarian labor rules, it was not possible, nor was it considered legitimate by Aukan people.

Labor and Christian Pilgrimage

The Deni Case Reconsidered: A Solution

In the case of the Deni, a missionary brought his own assumptions about work rules to a Brazilian Indian community. While he knew the Deni did not know his labor game, he expected that the Deni had a community system of labor, that the chief held community authority, and that redistribution of goods was a common practice. He hoped that the chief could evaluate the labor of villagers and pay them in accord with their work (see fig. 4.3). The Deni comprehended none of this but defined work in terms of objective tasks and rewards. To the Deni every work project is individually organized. The time spent, the level of individual effort, and the amount of reward are variable and subject to negotiation. The missionary's concern to pay hard workers more than casual workers was not their concern.

The labor game for the Deni is not rule-directed but individualist and goal-directed. Work and reward must be negotiated in each situation. I have observed Deni complaining about individuals who continue to borrow from them and do not return; however, they do not stop loaning. They merely complain and try to renegotiate their relationships with these individuals.

Is it possible to resolve such conflicts in a positive way rather than to go our separate ways? The answer to this question is yes, if missionaries are willing to change their expectations to mesh with the social environment of those with whom they work. This may be illustrated by relating Koop's solution of how to pay the Deni for work on the airstrip.

The solution allowed both the missionary and the Deni to work according to their own requirements and at the same time be satisfied with arrangements for pay. Koop needed to feel that the amount of money expended on his behalf produced the appropriate amount of labor from the people. The Deni did not understand his rules or his conception of work. They defined the work in terms of their personal goals.

The job had to be redefined in such a way that both Koop's goals and their goals were met. To discover a solution to this problem, we examined all Deni labor activities and found an

Figure 4.3
Koop and Deni Labor Assumptions

Authoritarian	**Hierarchist** *Koop's Assumptions* *Community labor* *Authority delegated to chief* *Standard wage rate*
Individual labor *Authority to organizer* *Standards negotiated* *Deni Assumptions* **Individualist**	**Egalitarian**

analogy in their practice of dividing a manioc field proportion-
ately among the men and women who shared in the labor of
clearing it. By dividing the airstrip into ten-meter segments and
assigning parcels to individuals, Koop distributed the work and
related the task to each individual's personal goals. He discovered from each individual what he or she hoped to earn. One
person selected a pair of blue jeans and a shirt, another selected
a couple of aluminum pans, and so on. If they asked for too
much, Koop offered what he felt was legitimate pay for the job.
Once the individual reward had been negotiated for each worker,
Koop explained what needed to be done to achieve the goal. By
redefining a job in terms of goals, the people proceeded with the
work and completed it to the satisfaction of everyone involved.
These negotiations led to ongoing satisfied relationships with
the people in the community.

What are the ramifications of the individualist social game
for moral standards? Missionaries will not find a series of Ten
Commandments that govern life. For example, Deni complain
about the bad behavior of people but do not see that behavior
in terms of a series of moral rules. Rather, they view that behavior as conflicting with their own goals. Such societies have been
mislabeled amoral. Rather, the norms of morality are negotiated on the basis of the requirements for members of the society to achieve their personal interests. The definition of moral
behavior is renegotiated, as are the work rules, when individuals engage in conflict with one another.

Perhaps the most practical rule for a society such as the Deni
is the Golden Rule: Do unto others as you would have others do
unto you. Because so many of their relationships and activities
are negotiated, they understand best the process of negotiation
and equal treatment in relationship to one another. A set of stan-
dardized rules about behavior does not fit with their understanding of how life and work should proceed. However, the
negotiation of relationships in terms of fairness is quite readily
understood and accepted.

The Bible and Labor

Some people come to the Scriptures seeking normative instructions with which they may solve conflicts like those des-

cribed. Some Bible teachers might choose the case study of Nehemiah to teach effective leadership and to show Aukan pastors why and how they should get with the program that the mission leader has chosen. Such a Bible study has limited relevance unless the teacher understands Jerusalem in the fifth century B.C. in terms of a corporate hierarchist social game. When Nehemiah proposed reconstruction of the wall, the people in their worldview understood and shared the shame that Nehemiah felt. They agreed that the task was both worthy and urgent and committed themselves to carry out this work in spite of opposition and danger. This case is a classic illustration of how tasks may be assigned to corporate groups and how work might be organized and directed by corporate leaders whose authority comes from their status within their respective groups. To apply the principles in Nehemiah to other social games without careful recontextualization can lead to false applications and destructive leadership training.

It is essential to understand that the case studies in Scripture reflect distinctive social games and worldviews and that both the cases and the contexts vary. For example, the case study of Jacob (Gen. 30:25–43) reflects an individualist game for labor. Jacob and Laban negotiate the matters of labor and wages. Jacob pleads with Laban to release him to return to his own homeland. Laban in return pleads with Jacob to stay and says, "Name your wages, and I will pay them" (v. 28). Divining that Jacob is bringing him good fortune, Laban seeks to capitalize on that advantage as long as possible. After they have agreed that Jacob will get the speckled, spotted, and dark-colored sheep and goats, Jacob uses magic and planned breeding to increase the size of his own herds (Gen. 30:37–39). Laban and Jacob compete with one another, each seeking to enhance his own wealth and to use the labor and resources of the other to assist in that effort.

In contrast, Jacob's son Joseph, who becomes ruler over all of Egypt, provides an excellent illustration of the bureaucratic authoritarian organization of labor (Gen. 47). Joseph uses the huge quantities of grain, stored up during the seven years of plenty, to extend the control of Pharaoh over all of Egypt. After the people of Egypt had used their money and livestock to buy grain, the text reports that Joseph bought all the land in Egypt for Pharaoh. "The Egyptians, one and all, sold their fields, because the famine was too severe for them . . . and Joseph reduced the people to servitude, from one end of Egypt to the other" (Gen. 47:20–21). In the organization that followed, one-fifth of the crops of Egypt belonged to Pharaoh and four-fifths were allocated to the laborers as food for themselves, their households, and their children. Joseph's success affects the descendants of both Egyptians and Israelites; in Exodus we find the Israelites serving as slave laborers for a descendent of Pharaoh, who authorizes foremen to force them to produce the bricks to meet a daily quota (Exod. 5). When Moses seeks to free the people, Pharaoh instructs the foremen to withhold the straw, forcing the people to gather stubble in the fields yet produce bricks at the same rate that they had done in previous days. The nomadic individualist herders from Canaan had been transformed into slave laborers, working by production quotas and work rules imposed upon them by authoritarian foremen in Pharaoh's bureaucracy.

The scriptural case that illustrates the collectivist egalitarian social game is found in the New Testament. Following the resurrection of Jesus, the disciples organize around egalitarian principles. The believing disciples, numbering about 120, gathered frequently for prayer. In a short time, the group enjoyed a remarkable degree of unity and collective interest. Peter initiated the decision to select a replacement for Judas, but the decision was accomplished by group prayer and the casting of lots. The outpouring of the Holy Spirit occurred when they were all gathered together in one place. The work of the early church emphasized collective action (Acts 2:42–47), with the apostles providing leadership for the new believers.

The Holy Spirit has anointed leaders to serve in social environments modeled after all four of the prototype social games. The details of these cases show that these leaders acted consistently and appropriately within the context of that historic social environment and worldview. Peter followed the first-among-equals leadership expectations of the egalitarian gathering of disciples, while Nehemiah acted with the compelling authority appropriate to the hierarchist structure of fifth-century Jerusalem. Each case provides an illustration of spiritually empowered leadership appropriate to the context in which it occurs.

Working for the Lord: The Metaphors of the Pilgrim

Scripture does not prescribe a particular social game or worldview. The Spirit of God calls believers to pilgrimage in whatever social game and environment they find themselves. This is an essential fact if we are to understand how to apply the teaching of Scripture to the practical questions of life in various social games of ministry. The theme of Scripture is not the restructuring of social environments into an ideal kingdom type but rather the application of metaphors of ministry or kingdom principles to ordinary working relationships.

Paul's message to hierarchist Greeks at Ephesus and Colosse compels new believers to rethink their relationships in the world. While Paul accepts the master-slave relationship as a given, he challenges both master and slave to redeemed relationships with one another. The slave is to work "with sincerity of heart and reverence for the Lord" (Col. 3:22); the master is to "provide your slaves with what is right and fair, because you know you also have a Master in heaven" (Col. 4:1). Paul reminds his readers that "anyone who does wrong will be repaid for his wrong, and there is no favoritism" (Col. 3:25). The central theme of Paul's message to masters and slaves is summed up in his command, "Whatever you do, work at it with all your heart, as working for the Lord, not for men, since you know you will receive an inheritance from the Lord as a reward. It is the Lord Christ you are serving" (Col. 3:23–24).

The text in Colossians and the parallel text in Ephesians 6:5–9 are not a rationale for particular structural relationships but rather an argument that those relationships in their natural social contexts must be redeemed. Paul challenges new believers to discharge the duties of their roles in family, community, and ministry as if they were working for the Lord and not for other people. This metaphor of submission to Christ and service to others pervades New Testament teaching on transformed labor relationships.

These texts take as given the existing structures and worldview of Greek or Jewish society, both of which are hierarchist social games. The texts do not justify the abuses and sins of the social environment but instead call Christians to be followers of Christ even in those abusive contexts. Peter (1 Peter 2:18) advises Jewish believers to submit even to harsh masters, recognizing the unjustness of their behavior. Peter calls them to a consciousness of God and to an endurance for the sake of the gospel. Peter uses Jesus as the illustrative example, noting how he did not retaliate when he suffered but rather entrusted himself to God. Peter sums up the purpose of suffering for the believer: "But rejoice that you participate in the sufferings of Christ, so that you may be overjoyed when his glory is revealed" (1 Peter 4:13).

The social norms of each type of social game serve to regulate the behavior of the members within that environment. As we have seen in our discussion, labor may be organized either by rule or by goal considerations and by priority given to individual or group demands. In each of the respective social games, people seek to control their own labor and the labor of others for personal and group advantage. Peter and Paul reject the priorities of personal and group advantage and call us to glorify God and work in his service. This may be accomplished in various ways, depending on the social game we encounter.

The Aukan church in Surinam (egalitarian) emphasizes that its members should work without pay. They hold up Colossians 3:23 as their motto and claim that they are working for the Lord. Serving the church is the primary group value. Individuals are measured in terms of their commitment to serving the Lord and his people. Senior men and women are rewarded with leadership roles in recognition of their years of faithful service.

In my church in southern California, we labor under a more corporate type of social organization (hierarchist). We have elected officers, paid staff, and many lay leaders. The board, the trustees, the deacons, and the Sunday school staff all have their respective roles and responsibilities. In our meetings we talk about job descriptions, tasks to be done, listening to the people, and support or lack of support of the congregation for the leaders. We typically recruit workers to fill particular tasks that we have identified as necessary for priority ministries. The reward typically given to the volunteer is that you have done your duty as a member and as a servant in the body of Christ. Occasionally people rally in collective excitement to support an all-church work day, to move a pastor into his new home, or to celebrate the success of the ministries of the members.

The Vineyard (individualist) has a loosely structured organization, individually spawned ministries, and temporary activity groups. The leaders emphasize the diverse interests of their members and promote various activities among them. The people have no need to know what others are doing, and the leaders coordinate many different activities. People gain their reward by exercising their gifts and celebrating together the work of the Holy Spirit in their midst.

In summary, each of these different church organizations has accepted the truth of Colossians 3:23, but each has contextualized this truth in terms of its respective social game. The Scriptures speak to people, people respond in context, and the Word powerfully transforms the church and its relationship to the world. Each congregation organizes believers to do the work of Christ, yet each conceptualizes the structure and reward of service in ways that reflect a select social game. At the same time each has responded to the gospel message and to the call of discipleship to Christ. All seek to discharge the duties of ministry (2 Tim. 4:5) as working for the Lord and not for people. When at times they look more like the world than like Jesus, it is because they have focused on the rules of the game rather than the metaphors of ministry found in Scripture.

5
Generosity and Exchange
The Stone of Stumbling in Interpersonal Relationships

Case Studies

Borrowing in America

During my teenage years in northern Ohio, I was socialized into a middle-class social world in which every individual owned all the essential items needed to live an ordinary life. Each of my neighbors had an automobile, a lawn mower, garden tools, and a ladder. These items were neither casually loaned nor easily borrowed, except from a special friend. I learned quickly that we should each have our own things and should not ask others for theirs. My neighbors emphasized by practice that we should be independent and manage our own economic affairs. We did not share money, nor did we share the objects of our material prosperity. If people borrowed tools, they were embarrassed to have to ask, and often they returned those items quickly so as to not to incur further obligation or to earn disapproval. People talked about those who borrowed as having a flaw in their character. Respectable people provided for their own needs and had no need for the help of others.

Attitudes of economic independence and reluctance to share and exchange with one another are quite common among Americans. Borrowing is carefully regulated, and individuals do it only to the extent that they can maintain their autonomy in relationships to others. Only the poorest must borrow from others. Borrowing is a measure of inadequacy in terms of achieving success and prosperity.

Individuals who are socialized in such an environment struggle with the strong expectations of reciprocity often found in other cultures in the world. Missionaries, anthropologists, and government workers who must live for extended periods of time in such cultures find them confusing at least and frustrating and trying at worst.

Borrowing in Yap

The people of the islands of Yap in the western Caroline Islands are brown-skinned, black-haired Micronesians, numbering approximately ten thousand in the 1990 census. I first lived in Yap from 1967 to 1969, doing research on traditional culture and political change, when Yap was an administrative district of the U.S. Trust Territory of the Pacific Islands. I returned to Yap in 1979–1980 to conduct research on the impact of thirty-five years of American administration and education on marriage and family relationships. Today these islands are part of Yap State in the Federated States of Micronesia, independent politically but under a free association agreement with the United States.

While the economy and material culture of the islands have changed much over the last thirty-five years, the fundamental features of the Yap social environment remain the same. Yapese people continue to place very high value on membership and obligation to traditional kin and village groups. They also have a highly developed traditional and contemporary hierarchy, with a strong, high grid social environment. Throughout this book the Yapese stories illustrate the hierarchist social game in a traditional and changing island culture (Lingenfelter 1975).

My experiences living with the people of Yap produced precisely the conflict alluded to. For Yapese people, borrowing is an ordinary part of life, and people turn frequently to their neighbors for material assistance. Soon after my arrival on Yap, my neighbors discovered the few tools and material possessions that I had brought with me. Shortly, one came and asked to borrow my motorbike; another came and asked for money; soon nearly every material possession that I owned had been the subject of a request to borrow. In every case, I either refused or gave reluctantly. I remember specifically the incident involving my hammer.

One day a young boy came and asked me if a neighbor on the other side of the village could borrow my hammer. Since this was early in my stay and I did not understand the rules, I said, "No problem!" I gave him the hammer, and he went on his way.

Several weeks passed. On one or two occasions I thought of using the hammer but realized that I had loaned it to this neighbor. One day, quite frustrated because I wanted a hammer, I caught sight of the same boy who happened to be passing my house and asked, "Whatever happened to my hammer?" When he answered that he did not know, I instructed him to go to that man, find my hammer, and bring it back to me. An hour or so later, the boy returned with a hammer. He told me it was not my hammer; it belonged to Tamag, who lived nearby. The boy said the handle on my hammer had been broken; some children were playing with the head and lost it. However, Tamag said I could use his hammer as long as I wanted it.

By that time I was not concerned about who owned the hammer, only that I had one to use for the task at hand. I used it for several days and then placed it in my house with my other tools. Taking a cue from the first borrower, I did not return it but waited to see what would happen. Several weeks later another little boy came to my house and asked if by chance I had "the" hammer. I said, "What do you mean, 'the' hammer?" He said, "Oh, the hammer that belongs to Tamag down the path." I confessed that I did have the hammer and told him that my hammer had been lost. The boy had been sent to borrow Tamag's hammer. Since Tamag had loaned the hammer to me, he sent this boy to my house. Recognizing that I was party to a growing string of exchanges, I gave it to him, and that was the last time I saw that particular hammer.

The people of Yap are generally willing to share what they have with others. One is not under obligation to return a borrowed object until the person who needs it calls for it. As long as I did not need a hammer, people felt no obligation to return it to my house. However, at the time when I did express need, the person who borrowed it helped me find a hammer that I could use.

This type of reciprocal borrowing is alien to middle-class American culture. The idea that something that I purchased might not be returned to me creates frustration, tension, and even animosity toward the borrower. Missionaries who take up residence in a social environment such as that on Yap struggle over the loss of tools and other objects because of values. Sometimes we accuse our neighbors of stealing rather than participate with them in a system of reciprocity according to the rules of their social world.

Given these differences in expectations, missionaries and nationals often not only do not understand one another but also build up feelings of hostility because of faulty expectations. I remember occasions when Yapese borrowed money from me. I looked for those persons for days afterward, expecting them to return the money. According to their values, the repayment need not occur for months or even years. Further, the repayment need not be in kind but rather might come in some other form or service. My middle-class American expectations are that repayment should be immediate and that the person who has received these goods becomes increasingly inferior to me the longer the payment is delayed.

Borrowing among the Deni

Within a few hours of my arrival in the jungle village of the Deni Indians in Brazil, I was unrolling my sleeping gear on the palm floor of a thatched-roof hut, when three Indian men walked up the ladder stairway and entered my domain. The owner of the house was absent temporarily from the village, and I had been granted permission to stay there. My guests sat down in a semicircle around my suitcase and began to talk with one another. Since I did not understand their language and they did not understand mine, we sat and looked at one another while they conversed. A few moments passed. One of the men then unlatched my suitcase and opened it. They crowded more closely and began to lift out the clothing, notebooks, and the bag of candy that I had tucked underneath my clothes. Soon they had taken complete inventory of all the private items in my suitcase and placed them back in the case. Leaving the lid open, one of the men walked over to a little shelf where I had placed my shaving kit, opened it, and began to sort through its contents. He took particular delight in my shampoo. He showed it to his friends and then slipped it into the pocket of his old missionary-barrel blue jeans. With that I let out a yell and ran to him to retrieve my shampoo. No longer silent, I declared in English that these were my things and they should not be messing in my private belongings. I retrieved the shampoo, placed it in the case, and closed it tightly. Then I went to the suitcase, closed the lid, latched it, and moved it away from them. They sat for a few moments grinning at one another, conversing further; then they dismissed themselves and departed. This introduction to Deni behavior and values taught me quickly that we had different concepts of private. I had much to learn.

A few days later, sitting on the open living verandah of my friends, the Koops, I observed a brief conversation between Mrs. Koop and a Deni woman who then left the house. Mrs. Koop told me the woman had asked if she could eat with us that evening. When I asked what her response had been, she, with tears in her eyes, said no. She explained how when they had first arrived, people asked, and they had allowed them to eat. Soon, half of the village was eating with them, and their food supplies were rapidly depleted. Deni came on a daily basis to ask them for various items of food that they had brought with them. Having planned for a period of two or three months, they knew the limits of their food stores and learned quickly that to give to anyone resulted in many more requests. Deciding that the welfare of their children was more important than generosity, they decided to not give food to the Deni.

This decision created strain for the Koops as well as frustration in their relationships with the people. The Koops felt a Christian obligation to be generous and caring for their neighbors, yet they saw the consequences of even small acts of generosity. The Deni seemed to have an insatiable appetite for their food and material goods and would ask and take until everything was gone.

The Koops did not know how the Deni felt about their refusal. After nearly a year of residing in the village, they still did not have a clear picture of Deni exchange relationships. One thing they did understand: Deni were aggressive in their pursuit of the material goods and food that they brought with them. Yet for the most part they did not steal from the Koops, and when they were told no, they accepted that decision and continued to be friendly and open.

The Deni adapted quickly to the system of exchange established by the translator. He offered material goods in return for meat and contributed coffee on their feast days. They made artifacts that they brought to him in exchange for material goods. He took these artifacts to the city and sold them at market prices to recover his costs. In this way he attempted to serve them, helping them meet their need for clothing and other goods.

Notwithstanding, my friends felt that at times they were un-Christian in their attitudes about food. In their hearts they desired to give to the Deni, yet because the Deni would take all that they had, they knew they could not do so. They did not understand the rules of Deni exchange relationships and struggled to know how best to work with them.

Asking and Social Exchange

Middle-class American, Yap, and Deni societies play very different social games on the subject of borrowing and exchange. In each of these societies, people have specific expectations as to how material goods and food should be shared and distributed among people.

Every society has specific values and expectations with regard to managing wealth. In some societies personal wealth is desired and approved by the members. In others, people employ leveling mechanisms to keep one individual from gaining more wealth than others in their group. In still other societies, people have inherited rules of hierarchy that prescribe the flow of goods to specific individuals who occupy positions of power and may use that power to gain personal wealth.

The goal of this chapter is to discover what patterns characterize exchange and distribution in the four prototype social games and how these patterns vary as they are elaborated in specific societies and cultures around the world. We shall also identify the patterns of exchange and distribution that are typical in America and see how these patterns produce value orientations that, when carried into another social environment, may produce conflict and confrontation with others. Conflict arising out of misunderstanding of values about exchange often becomes a stone of stumbling in interpersonal relationships for Christian workers in cross-cultural settings.

High Grid—Asking Is Humiliating

While the Yapese and I had different values in regard to giving, we shared the feeling that asking is humiliating. The fact that my neighbors sent a young boy to ask for my hammer reflects this value. In high grid social games, the one who asks is always lower than the one who gives. The giver occupies a position of superiority and power over the receiver. The only way that one can restore the balance in the relationship is to repay the debt. Repayment in a high grid social game restores equality between the persons involved. In my experience on Yap, persons in my debt avoided contact with me if at all possible. They were ashamed to meet me in public, knowing my expectation for repayment of their obligation. Only after the debt was paid could we engage in normal social relationships again.

The Yapese sometimes engage in competitive giving with one another. On occasion political rivals seek to outgive one another in ceremonial exchanges. While this is not typical of my urban middle-class society, the neighbor who has the newest lawn mower, the best equipment, or the highest-priced car is thought to be superior to the neighbor who owns lower-quality goods.

Low Grid—Asking Is Negotiating

The case study of the Deni illustrates graphically the individualist, low grid social game. Not only are the Deni not humiliated, but also they ask boldly for whatever they desire. They take no offense when what they seek is not granted but consider the low risk of asking worth the effort. The Deni engage in a series of negotiating requests with missionaries and their Brazilian neighbors.

In a low grid social game, the giver is in competition with the asker. Each is struggling to gain advantage in a social environment where individual or group autonomy is highly valued. The Deni expect that their Brazilian patrons will have some competitive advantage in their mutual relationships. They see the missionary through the same eyes. All of the individuals in their social environment compete for similar or shared resources. The Deni see the giver as one from whom they should take an opportunity for personal gain. They also recognize that givers will serve their personal interests; they therefore have little animosity toward others when their request is denied. Asking and giving are part of a negotiating process in which to give or to receive holds prospect for longer-term individual gain.

In this same manner, repayment in a low grid social game often entails profit to the giver. The Brazilian patron relationship to the Deni is a graphic example. When a Deni visits his patron's home he expects to be fed, and he will ask for clothing, aluminum utensils, and other items that he wishes to add to his personal wealth. The patron will give to the extent that he believes he can induce the Deni to repay him. Often the Brazilian must go after the Deni worker and even coerce him to repay his debt. When the Deni does join him to work, the Brazilian will get as much labor from him as is possible under the circumstances. Usually the patron profits from Deni labor. The Deni and the Brazilians recognize this and continue to work the system to their mutual advantage when possible.

High Group—Asking Places the Group at Risk

In a strong group social game, individuals are not easily isolated from the context and demands of their group. When an individual asks for valued goods or services, the debt may not be only personal; it may also accrue to the social group. In such a social environment, the members of the group see the requests of individuals to outsiders as placing their group at risk. As a consequence, the group exerts significant pressure on its members to avoid seeking assistance from competing groups. Within the group reciprocity is often general, and members may seek all the assistance they need from their fellows. To request assistance of another group, however, is deemed risky and diminishes the public image of the strength of the group. For example, a group of Aukan villagers sought to build an airstrip on village land. They sent a delegation to an up-river village to request the use of a bulldozer controlled by the regional headman. They did so knowing that the request would probably be denied. Yet they were willing to take the risk knowing that without the bulldozer the airstrip would be an impossible task for them. The headman rejected their request, and the leaders refused to consider going to him again. The social cost of their first request was already more than they wanted to risk; they did so in part because they could not appeal to the government for help without first asking the regional headman.

In the reverse situation, a group that gives generously acquires significant social capital through the exchange. In the Aukan illustration, if the regional headman had granted the use of the bulldozer, he would have increased his social standing and power over the requesting village. By refusing them he not only humiliated them but also limited his credit for future support. A generous group in a high group social game gains significant social power and influence.

Because asking places a group at risk, repayment is compulsory for the members. There is never a question of whether the group should repay but only the question of when, how much, and through what means. The group works to remove whatever risk may have been entailed by asking or receiving material wealth from others.

Low Group—Asking Is Advantageous

In a weak group social game, the person who asks is seeking individual gain. Lacking the constraints of group membership and binding social networks with others, the person asking risks only a specific relationship. In Honoré Balzac's *Eugénie Grandet* (1833), Eugénie's miser father operates in a weak group social environment. For Monsieur Grandet asking is a game he plays with all of his friends and patrons to outwit them and to obtain from them some economic advantage.

The story of Grandet is classic with regard to the factors of giving and repayment. Grandet refuses to give to anyone, including his wife and daughter. The family lives on an extremely sparse allowance, eating a diet of bread and water and minuscule portions of meat and vegetables, in spite of the fact that Grandet is an extremely wealthy man. Grandet views any giving as an economic loss and seeks to minimize every possible loss of his funds.

Grandet repays only when the funds are demanded of him. When his brother dies in bankruptcy, Grandet arranges with the creditors to pay off his brother's debts if they allow him to take over the assets. The creditors agree to this strategy in hopes of reducing their losses. However, Grandet pays them as little as is necessary, drawing profit from the assets while keeping these creditors at bay.

The case of Monsieur Grandet is one in which social values other than his own play a minimal role in his life and relationships. He alienates his fellow townspeople, his fellow winemakers, and all of those with whom he does business or has social relationships. He does so at will, recognizing that their primary interest in him is also to gain advantage over his resources. While this is an extreme case, it clearly illustrates the factors of exchange in a weak group social game.

Conflicts about Exchange

Perhaps the most common frustration experienced by cross-cultural workers is how to play the exchange game in a host culture. Missionaries often feel pressured by nationals to give goods and money to them. Many missionaries ask how much they should give, when they should give, and what should they expect in terms of repayment. It is difficult to lay down a set of guidelines that will work in the diverse cultures and social environments in which missionaries work. As is evident in the two case studies that opened this chapter, a missionary in Yap would experience extremely different values and expectations than would a missionary among the Deni in Brazil.

The prototype social games, while not foolproof, provide a place to begin. By exploring these four distinctive social games (see fig. 5.1), we may compare and contrast exchange behaviors and through this process sort out those values that are significant in the cultural setting where we work. The two case studies of conflict that follow illustrate how this model may be used to understand the differing behavior of nationals and to

Figure 5.1
Social Games and Exchange Priorities

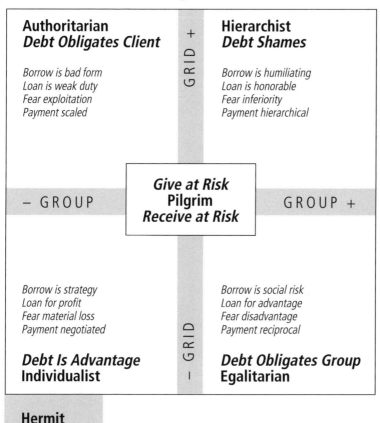

Authoritarian
Debt Obligates Client

Borrow is bad form
Loan is weak duty
Fear exploitation
Payment scaled

GRID +

Hierarchist
Debt Shames

Borrow is humiliating
Loan is honorable
Fear inferiority
Payment hierarchical

Give at Risk
Pilgrim
Receive at Risk

– GROUP   GROUP +

Borrow is strategy
Loan for profit
Fear material loss
Payment negotiated

Borrow is social risk
Loan for advantage
Fear disadvantage
Payment reciprocal

Debt Is Advantage
Individualist

GRID –

Debt Obligates Group
Egalitarian

Hermit

develop more effective strategies for coping with these distinctive values.

Gifts and Pay in Yap: A Hierarchist Game

When I returned to Yap in 1970, I purchased a number of gifts to give to people who had assisted me during the first two years of my field work there. Some of these people were part of the household and lineage in which I had lived for that two-year period. They were like my kinsmen and considered me a part of their group. Other gifts were for people who lived in other areas and by whom I was considered an outsider.

Within my community, people who had become part of my family received my gifts and expressed their appreciation without further comment. However, the response of some old men in another district to my gifts caught me by surprise. The oldest man, to whom I had given a watch, asked me pointedly how much it cost. He did not know that I had purchased a cheap watch at K-Mart or what the price of the watch might be. While I did not have much money, I knew that Yapese were particular about the value of things. I was embarrassed to tell him the price, thinking it would communicate that our friendship was of little value. In fact the friendship was of great value to me, but living on a limited income and having been reared in a frugal family, I felt constrained in the amount of money that I should spend for these gifts.

My elderly friend insisted on knowing the price. As I resisted he became angry with me and could not understand why I should refuse to tell him. One of the other men explained to me that if he did not know the price he would not know what his obligation was and how to repay me. I refused to tell him the price of the watch, which created a considerable strain on our relationship over the next several days.

As I reflect upon this situation twenty years later, I understand now that his anxiety about obligation grew out of the hierarchist social game of Yapese village life. Since I was not a member of his group my gift to him, without stated price, placed him and his social group at risk. He felt obligated to pay me, but because of my refusal he had no idea what his obligation was.

My response was incomprehensible to him. Any self-respecting Yapese would have made it clear what the price of the object was so the members of the other group would know their obligation and risk.

My relationship with my Yapese family and neighbors was quite different. I had been accepted as a member of that group, and we had engaged in a series of generalized exchanges with one another. They had provided land, food, and a car during my stay on Yap, and I had returned full support for two of their children to attend school in the United States. We had developed an open credit/open trust relationship. Our mutual giving solidified our relationship as insiders, and the exchanges between us had become generalized reciprocity. We did not keep track of our obligations but expected that over a long period of time things would balance out. This type of exchange is acceptable between insiders in a group, but it is not possible between people who are outsiders.

In 1979–1980 we returned to Yap a third time to continue our research. On this occasion I had financial support through a research grant and also had a better-paying job in the state university where I taught. The grant provided funds to pay for Yapese laborers to support me in the research project. For this research I recruited a team of ten Yapese men who worked as census takers and interviewers. Having observed Yapese in hourly wage labor, I knew that paying by the hour would be disastrous. I arranged to pay them for the completed forms that they returned to me. Every week or two as a man completed census surveying in his area, he would bring his completed forms to my office in town. After checking these materials, I would pay him for the work completed.

One evening one of the census takers came to my office and asked if he could talk to me privately. It was evident that he had been drinking and that he was under stress. He began by saying that he was in a predicament and needed someone to help him. The sudden death of one of his relatives required money for funeral expenses. Explaining that he had no time to do more census forms, he asked me to give him an advance on his pay for the next two weeks. Understanding the situation, I asked how much he needed and gave him the money. He was very appreciative, thanked me, and left immediately to join a friend waiting for him in the car.

I did not see this man again for more than a month. One day I happened to see him with another man passing by at the main crossroads in the government center. Expecting that he might disappear if he saw me, I moved quickly to greet him and to ask how things were going. He apologized for not seeing me and said that he had been very busy and hoped that I would not be angry. I assured him that I was not angry; however, I worried that he might give up his census work and that I would need to find someone else to do it. He assured me that he had several completed census forms at home, but he had not had time to bring them to me. A few days later he came with his census work, yet not enough to cover the advance that I had given to him. After I checked these forms he asked me for another advance. What should I do?

This dilemma is typical for missionaries and research employers in places like Yap. In the hierarchist social games, the missionary or the anthropologist occupies a superior role to the workers that they employ. In a hierarchist system, the inferior members look to higher ranks for patronage as well as compensation. If I had been Yapese, I would not question his worthiness to receive the extra help. However, Americans communicate negative vibrations much more overtly than do Yapese of similar strata and rank. I had made him uncomfortable when I gave him the first advance, and he felt embarrassed and demotivated to continue his work. He had anticipated that his relationship with me was deep enough that patronage was a reasonable expectation. I had communicated to him that the advance was conditional.

By that time in my work with Yapese I had begun to understand this intuitively. For me, it was more important to keep him as a trained census worker than to worry about the amount of money that I had advanced. I told him how much I appreciated the work that he had done and that he could consider the advance a gift from me to help support his need at the time of the funeral. I then paid him for the census forms that he had brought that day, which more than met his financial expectations and need at that time.

The confusion between the two of us arose from our different expectations about exchange. From my point of view, he should receive material benefit only as direct compensation for his labor. From his point of view, we had a relationship that was more than employer-employee; I had become part of his social game, which prescribed not only payment for labor but also patron gift transactions. Once I understood and acted upon this knowledge, he and the other census workers served much more effectively in our cooperative work relationship.

Helping in Surinam: An Egalitarian Game

The egalitarian social games of the Saramaccans and Aukaners in Surinam create quite a different set of expectations. Young Saramaccan men are unabashed in their economic requests. As I bathed in a stream each morning, I was inundated with requests for my watch, my shorts, and my shirt. These young teenagers declared that I was wealthy, that I had many more pants and shorts back in Paramaribo, and surely I should help them by sharing what I had. I argued that I had only two pair of shorts, and they replied that they had only one. I said my mother-in-law had given me the watch, and they said she could buy me another one. No amount of explanation could convince them that I was anything other than stingy. I did not give them my shorts, my shirt, or my watch, but they were undaunted in their requests for these objects.

A few weeks later in an Aukan village, the elders of the village asked us if we would help them to obtain financial support to build an airstrip. As my colleague and I discussed these matters with them, we sensed a deep suspicion about our motives. One of our objectives was to learn more about the leadership structure and process of the Aukan village. When we tried to ask these questions, they responded by asking, "Why do you want to know?" Our dialogue again was one of negotiation. They sought reassurances from us that we would indeed help them, and they refused to help us until we could produce something of concrete value. Finally my colleague and I sat with a group of men and drafted a letter that communicated their specific wants to a government official in Paramaribo. After that letter was completed and signed by the village captain, the men were much more cooperative, responding to our questions and interests.

What are the variables in these two different situations? Both Aukan and Saramaccan villagers play egalitarian social games. The young men negotiating for my watch, shorts, and shirt challenged me as an outsider. They gave nothing to me and tried to get as much from me as they could. Since I sought nothing from them, we engaged one another in cheerful banter and a contest to see what we might gain out of the exchange. With the elderly men in the Aukan village the stakes were much more serious. My colleague and I wanted to learn something about them, and they refused to teach us until they obtained a significant benefit for themselves. Guarded in their interactions with us, they closed us out until we could demonstrate to them our helpfulness by communicating their need to a key government official. I also promised to send them two come-alongs, a winch-type tool that they could use to pull out tree stumps. While they were skeptical that I would deliver, they accepted my promise as of potential value to them. I did in fact mail those tools to Surinam upon my return to the United States.

In both of these village situations, the young and the old operated from an egalitarian social game, emphasizing equal distribution of wealth and high commitment to the group. The young men asserted that we had more than we needed and we should share it with them. The old men expressed the same idea but in different terms. They denied us the information we wanted until we proved our commitment to help them.

Pilgrim Biblical Principles: Freedom in Giving and Receiving

These case studies illustrate how cross-cultural workers struggle with different social expectations for giving and receiving. Most Christian leaders have internalized biblical warnings about stinginess (Prov. 11:24; 28:27) and admonitions to guard against greed (Luke 12:15; Eph. 5:3). At the same time, missionary and national leaders often remain in bondage to the values and fears of their social games. While these social games are useful and good, they have not been designed to create disciples of Christ. Rather, they are systems structured to control greed, to regulate economic exchange, and to enable individuals to calculate interest and personal gains and losses within a social context. As systems to regulate and control individual behavior, they protect members of the society from the excesses of others, yet they do not lead people to the freedom and joy promised in the Lord Jesus Christ.

Fear in Giving and Receiving

Because these social games of exchange are designed to protect public values of good and to control deviant behaviors of individuals within the social environment, the standards within the culture usually address human fears of loss and exploitation. These standards define a range of appropriate behavior for giving and receiving upon which people should act and against which behavior is measured.

The greatest source of anxiety for a Yapese person is not in giving but in receiving. To receive is humiliating. It places the person in a subordinate role to the giver. The hierarchist village game in Yapese society places great value on generosity and gives high esteem to people who are extremely generous. Those who ask too frequently or show eagerness to get their share of goods being distributed are scorned as beggars and slothful. The persons who refuse to give are stigmatized as stingy. People who are successful openly deny their wealth and practice public generosity to reduce social criticism. At the same time, poor relatives often besiege them as inexhaustible sources for unmet wants and needs. Many prosperous Yapese have locked boxes where they hide valuables. They fear those who would surely ask, if they only knew.

The individualist Deni, in contrast, have no fear about receiving. Living in a highly competitive environment, they fear that others will use coercive force against them in the negotiating process. They fear the loss of profit from their efforts; they fear the loss of advantage in their relationship to others; they fear the power that others hold and may use against them; they fear the random forces of society and nature in which they experience feast and famine, good health and misfortune, or good talk and open conflict. They have no qualms about accumulating goods and wealth through exploitation. They eagerly receive from any who will give to them, and they are bold to ask. At the same time, they give only when pressed by others or when they believe giving will yield a profitable return or protection from some future disaster.

The egalitarian Aukan fear that someone will get ahead of them in the competition for resources and wealth. They despise anything that promotes inequality and assert their interest to gain a fair share of whatever is available to the group. They calculate relationships in terms of social debt and personal gain. Individuals within a group press one another to give for the group good. Within the Aukan church this is termed giving to the Lord. In their relationships with outsiders, the Aukan give only if they believe a return is assured. Afraid of being exploited and exposed to economic loss, they punish offenders by public exposure of their behavior and, if they are unrepentant, exclude these people from the group.

Western Christian workers commonly fear that they will be exploited by other-culture neighbors. Growing up in individualist or authoritarian families, they have learned to view their economic resources as scarce and to be conserved. They believe that each person is responsible for careful management of those resources and for personal welfare. As a consequence, when they are asked to give, they question whether what they give will be used wisely and if the person asking will exploit them or their resources. When neighbors ask for money, many fear they may exhaust their scarce resources. Others feel that giving unconditionally does not teach neighbors responsible behavior, and conversely, they are reluctant to receive gifts. Taught from their youth to be self-sufficient and independent, they believe that receiving substantive gifts from others casts a negative reflection upon their ability to provide for themselves. Many resist asking for material help from other-culture neighbors, fearing further reciprocal obligations. Finally, some fear that nationals do not respect them as persons but only as a source of money or material things. Feeling demeaned by the asking and giving, they see the resulting relationships tainted by low material motivation and interest.

Freedom to Give at Risk

For the Christian pilgrim, Scripture assures us that followers of Jesus Christ may be free from the anxieties that surround material life and resources. "Give to the one who asks you, and do not turn away from the one who wants to borrow from you" (Matt. 5:41). "So do not worry, saying, 'What shall we eat?' or 'What shall we drink?' or 'What shall we wear?' . . . But seek first his kingdom and his righteousness, and all these things will be given to you as well" (Matt. 6:31–33). We have also been taught to give out of our abundance or our poverty to the Lord. We have been challenged to "bring the whole tithe into the storehouse," and we have heard the promise from God, "see if I will not throw open the floodgates of heaven and pour out so much blessing that you will not have enough room for it" (Mal. 3:10). Yet we have been so conditioned by the standards and practice of our social games that we doubt the truth of Scripture and find it very difficult to live by it.

Many other passages in Scripture present similar challenges. Proverbs declares that the generous will prosper (11:25) and be blessed (22:9). Isaiah 58:10 addresses the issue of fear of losing personal prosperity for the sake of the poor: "If you spend yourselves in behalf of the hungry and satisfy the needs of the oppressed, then your light will rise in the darkness, and your night will become like the noonday." While we desire the blessing and glory of God, we fear the cost of pilgrimage and hold to the standards and rules of our social games. Our social games rob us of the freedom given to us in God's Word: liberation from anxiety about material things and the desire and joy to give at risk, testing God's capacity to give in return. The Christian worker who lives the life of pilgrimage defined in these passages finds freedom from anxiety about eating, drinking, and clothing and experiences the opening of the floodgates of heaven promised in the Book of Malachi.

The national Christian leader faces the same dilemma as the missionary. Fears about loss, exploitation, social debt, and humiliation inhibit national believers from embarking upon the pilgrimage of faith. However, those who have responded to the scriptural message have discovered that God is faithful. A friend related the story of a missionary working among the Dayaks in

Borneo. This missionary challenged the Dayaks to bring their
chickens and other food resources to God, for redistribution to
the poor and to those who had dedicated themselves to ministry.
After many people acted in simple obedience to this command,
they harvested and marketed a rice crop surplus beyond anything they had experienced before. By their obedience they discovered the truth of Proverbs 28:27: "He who gives to the poor
will lack nothing."

Freedom to Receive at Risk

Jesus said, "Give, and it will be given to you. A good measure,
pressed down, shaken together and running over, will be poured
into your lap. For with the measure you use, it will be measured
to you" (Luke 6:38). This metaphor is as much about receiving
as it is about giving. Receiving is an important part of the
exchange process. The missionary or the national who rejects a
gift because of the fear of humiliation, manipulation, or being
obligated to others loses a significant part of the blessing of God.
Jesus says the "good measure . . . will be poured into your lap."
To reject the pouring from God because of the social expectations that may come with it deprives the believer of material
blessing and of joy and freedom in Christ. The Christian pilgrim
has both the freedom to give at risk, and to receive at risk. These
are foundational kingdom principles by which our lives and the
lives of others may be transformed.

To receive at risk is a central tenet of our faith. The Gospels
and the epistles declare that our salvation in Christ is a gift of
God, something for which we cannot pay or work; we do not
have anything of value that God would want, and we must accept
his gift as an unconditional work of grace (Eph. 2:8–10). Our
first act of obedience as believers is to accept the gift of salvation in Jesus Christ. Yet we receive that gift at risk. God demands
our obedience and service. Our obedience of faith establishes a
pattern of relationship in Christ that should follow into our material life.

In three of the five social games, people are cautious about
receiving gifts and are careful to remove obligations of debt
because of the social and economic consequences. Only hermits

and individualists accept indebtedness openly. Individualists use debt to extend their personal acquisitions with an intent to compete and exploit. In all social games people employ debt primarily for selfish individual or group advantage rather than for the good of others.

To receive at risk in the biblical context implies a willingness to be humiliated, obligated, or even exploited by being in debt to others. The Christian pilgrim is willing to take the client rather than the patron role, as Jesus illustrated by his receiving the support of prominent Jewish women (Luke 8:1–3). National leaders often cast missionaries in the role of benefactors, having resources far beyond those available locally. Missionaries frequently retain the authority and power that belongs to a benefactor, and avoid reciprocal arrangements that might make nationals benefactors to us. In his final meeting with the Twelve, Jesus cautioned them against this very thing, calling them to be as those who serve at the table rather than benefactors (Luke 22:25–27).

Addressing Our Fears

The difficulty we have applying kingdom principles may be traced directly to fear. People teach their children what to fear and how to respond appropriately. Asking, giving, and receiving are actions that entail social risk, which in turn creates fear and anxiety among those at risk. The challenge of pilgrimage is to directly address these fears, to practice giving at risk and receiving at risk.

How does the Christian worker cope with the many people who knock at the door and ask for money or other material help? Instead of seeing these people as annoyances, we may view every person who comes as an opportunity for relationship and for sharing the gospel. Giving money or material things should never be a brief transaction. If we do not have time to talk at that moment, we may ask them to return at another time when we are free. It is helpful to ask people to explain their needs. We in turn may explain to them why we have come, how God has provided for us, and what our responsibilities are as stewards of

God's provision. We must understand their social game and their expectations. After understanding their fears and encouraging them toward faith in God to provide, we may minister to them through a gift or a loan. The opportunity to give is an opportunity for relationship and for witness; when we neglect taking time to talk about the transaction, we have wasted an important opportunity for witness.

Another issue for the Christian worker is the question, Whose money, mine or God's? All that we have belongs to the Lord, yet some of us have difficulty putting this truth into practice. We become anxious about our level of support and worry that too many gifts or loans will place us in financial jeopardy. A helpful technique may be to set aside a portion of financial support to be given to people who have need. Making the distribution of such funds a matter of personal prayer, the worker who gives should acknowledge openly that the gift is from a fund that belongs to God. The debt is to God and not to the giver, who is merely the steward.

Finally, it is helpful to remember that relationships must be reciprocal, in spite of our fear of obligation; if the giver never asks or receives, the relationship becomes one of domination and subordination. Christian workers must learn to ask for things they do not necessarily want or need (having been taught to be self-reliant) to allow their national friends to repay them. One of my friends working in the Philippines learned to ask others for help and in becoming dependent formed relationships deeper than those in her own family. Those friends have also become brothers and sisters in Christ.

In summary, the good news proclaimed by Christ is that we are pilgrims, empowered to freedom from the fears and selfish interests approved in our cultural system and social game. While our social games and cultural bias bring regulation and reason to economic relationships, by and in themselves they rob the believer of the freedom offered in Christ. This is not a freedom from work, not an encouragement to depend upon others for our food and shelter; Paul rebukes the Thessalonians sharply for that attitude (2 Thess. 3:6–15). Rather, the promises of God offer freedom from anxiety about material resources, freedom from fear about exploitation, humiliation, and social debt, and freedom to give and receive in the work of Christ. When we com-

mit ourselves to bless the poor, to feed the hungry, to share with
those who are in need, and to express our devotion to our Lord
Jesus Christ, we are assured of light in our lives, of provision for
our needs, and of receiving the measure that we have given to
others, "a good measure, pressed down, shaken together and
running over . . . poured into your lap."

6

Authority and Family
The Foundation of Social Order

Case Studies

Jacob

The case study of Jacob is presented in Genesis 25–31. The biblical account does not provide all of the ethnographic details of the life and family relationships of people at that time in Hebrew history. However, many of the domestic details presented in the text provide interesting insights into the nature of marriage, domestic labor, parent-child relationships, and aspects of family authority. The households of Isaac, Laban, and Jacob are variants of the individualist family game.

The story begins with an account of the births of Jacob and Esau. At their birth, the boys are described as having distinct personalities. As they grow up, Esau chooses to spend his early life with his father in the open country, while Jacob lives with his mother among the tents. Esau becomes a skilled hunter, while Jacob learns to care for the flocks and cook. Jacob and Esau are described as competitors. Jacob, relying on his skill as a herdsman and a cook, succeeds in negotiating from his famished brother, Esau, the rights to inherit the property of the firstborn from their father. Jacob and Rebekah use the skills of slaughter, cooking, and sewing to disguise Jacob. He deceives his father Isaac, and steals the blessing of the firstborn from Esau. The text describes these two men as competitors from the moment of their birth, and the individualist social game of their household encouraged that competition and independence.

Both Jacob and Esau spent forty years with their parents, living and working as members of their household. Esau arranged his own marriages with local Canaanite women. His choice was not pleasing to his mother and father, and he married without their permission or support. Jacob, who was more easily influenced, obeyed Isaac's directive to go to his uncle Laban's home in the hills of Syria and find a wife among his kinsmen there. When Esau heard of this, he took a third wife, the daughter of his uncle Ishmael, his father's half-brother.

While the text tells us nothing about Esau's relationship to his wife's parents, the story of Jacob is much more detailed. Laban offered to pay Jacob for working with the flocks. Jacob requested marriage with Laban's daughter Rachel and agreed to wait for seven years of bride service. Laban exercised his authority as father-in-law over Jacob for the seven years. When the time was completed, Laban gave his oldest daughter, Leah, rather than the girl he had promised. Laban had the upper hand since he was the father of the girls and controlled their marriages. Jacob agreed to work seven more years, and a week later he was allowed to take Rachel as his second wife. After almost twenty years of working for his father-in-law, Jacob negotiated a share of Laban's herds. Laban agreed to give Jacob the speckled and spotted lambs and goats, and Jacob used selective breeding to enhance his personal wealth.

The patterns in Jacob's family of birth are continued in his relationships with his wives and his children. Rachel and Leah engaged in competition with one another over who could bear the most children. Rachel used Jacob's love for her to keep Leah from having sexual access to her husband. Leah used her son, Reuben, who brought to her mandrakes, a fertility plant, to bargain with Rachel to gain sexual access to Jacob. The boys served as co-laborers with their mother and their father. Jacob gave his sons responsibility over his speckled herd while he took care of Laban's flocks. As we follow Jacob and his sons in later chapters in Genesis, we find the sons exercising much independent power, making their own decisions as Jacob and Esau did before them.

Jacob planned an escape from his father-in-law (Gen. 31). When Laban discovered that Jacob had departed with his wives, children, and herds, he set out in pursuit with his sons and a small army. Once again Jacob engaged in a process of negotiation to placate his angry uncle and defended himself against the accusation that one of his party had stolen Laban's gods. Rachel, Laban's younger daughter, had stolen the idols yet was successful in hiding them in her saddle bags.

Zachariah and Elizabeth, Mary and Joseph

The most extensive data in the New Testament come from three accounts in the Gospel of Luke: Zachariah, Elizabeth, and the birth of John the Baptist; Mary, Joseph, and the birth of Jesus; and the parable of the prodigal son. While the intent of these texts is not to provide an ethnographic account of family life, the details in them supply data from which we may answer questions about the structuring of authority, the organization of labor, and regulations surrounding marriage in first-century Jewish families. In striking contrast to the families of Isaac and Jacob, these families play a variant of the hierarchist social game.

The importance of genealogy for Jewish families is illustrated in both the Gospel of Luke and the Gospel of Matthew. Elizabeth and Zachariah are listed as descendants of Aaron (Luke 1:5) and Mary and Joseph as descendants of David in the tribe of Judah. The genealogies recount a line of patrilineal descent, and the text portrays the men as having primary authority in family relationships. Zachariah decides what his son is to be named (Luke 1:57–63). Joseph makes key decisions—whether or not to marry his betrothed, Mary; where they should go when they are threatened by Herod; and where they should ultimately settle.

While little information is given on the relationship between parents and children, the few clues that we find show children clearly subject to the authority of their parents. When Jesus is discovered in the temple by his parents (Luke 2:48–51) he accepts the rebuke of his mother. The text says, "He went down to Nazareth with them and was obedient to them" (v. 51). At the wedding at Cana in Galilee, Jesus' mother asks him to assist the host when the wine is gone, and Jesus responds to her request. Jesus illustrates obedience to the Jewish custom of lifelong subjection to parents. Yet this subjection was not always consistent with the calling that Jesus had from his Father. At the marriage in Cana, Jesus gently rebukes his mother: "My time has not come" (John 2:4).

With regard to family decisions and economic relationships the extended family appears to play an important role in first-century Jewish society. This is illustrated most graphically in the story of John the Baptist. Mary came to see her cousin Elizabeth and spent significant time with her before the birth of her baby. After Elizabeth gave birth to John, the neighbors and relatives attempted to influence Elizabeth's apparent decision to name the boy John. The relatives, who appealed to Zachariah with regard to this decision, were astonished when he wrote "his name is John." The third incident that shows the importance of the extended family is when Mary and Joseph took Jesus to Jerusalem. As they were returning to Nazareth, they thought that Jesus was in the company of their relatives who were traveling with them. These cases suggest that the role of the extended family was to provide mutual support and to give input on decisions that affected individuals within the group.

With regard to economic affairs in the family, Jewish families gave priority to the eldest child. This is most graphically illustrated in the story of the prodigal son (Luke 15:11–32) in which the younger son sought his portion of the estate and his father granted the request. The estate was held jointly by the father and the elder son (Luke 15:31); the younger son was given a designated share of the inheritance (v. 12). After the younger son squandered his portion of the inheritance, he was welcomed back to his father's house as a member, rather than a slave, much to the displeasure of his elder brother. At the same time, the father did not further divide the inheritance; he affirmed the rights of the elder son to all of his property. The younger son was welcomed back to the family, but the inheritance that he had squandered was not restored.

The concept of duty is often used to characterize relationships in Jewish family and society. Zachariah is described in Luke 1:8–10 as a man who had assigned duties in the temple because of his particular place in the genealogy of the family of Aaron. Joseph, as he considered the untimely pregnancy of his betrothed, decided to do his duty and set her aside quietly until he was persuaded otherwise by the Holy Spirit. In the story of the prodigal son, the elder brother became angry because he had been a model son, always performing his duty to his father; his father's welcome for his profligate brother offended his sense of justice. He perceived it as an insult to one who had been obedient and responsible according to the expectations of the culture (Luke 15:28–30). From this evidence we may characterize relationships between parents and children in these Jewish families by a sense of duty, obligation, and reciprocity.

These first-century families were careful to do everything according to Jewish law. Luke records how Joseph and Mary took the child Jesus to the temple on the eighth day to have him circumcised and to go through the purification rituals for Mary specified in the law of Moses. Luke is careful to point out that only after they had done everything required by the law of the Lord did they return to Galilee in the town of Nazareth (Luke 2:39).

Marriage in first-century Jewish families carried many of the same attributes described in the Old Testament historical books. Luke records the fact that Mary was pledged to be married to Joseph, an arrangement typically made between families in preparation of the marriage of their children. Mary and Joseph and Zachariah and Elizabeth married members of their tribe. Arranged marriages remained a typical pattern among New Testament Christians, as is evidenced by Paul's instructions in 1 Corinthians 7:36–38. The role of the family in the matter of marriage is evidenced by the practice of widow inheritance, illustrated in the discussion between the Sadducees and Jesus in Matthew 22:23–33.

To sum up, the authority structure of Jewish families in the New Testament period shows a strong commitment to corporate family relationships, the hierarchist social game (see fig. 6.1). The father in the family had ultimate authority. Family activities were regulated by the Mosaic law and by formal duties spelled out in customary practice. The eldest son was the heir of the family estate and held the right of succession to the role of his father. Marriages were arranged, and the corporate family had a long-term interest in the activities of the children. Once a woman married into a family group she belonged to that group. Should she become a widow, men in the group had the responsibility to provide for her—even to the point of producing children.

Figure 6.1
Family Social Games in Scripture

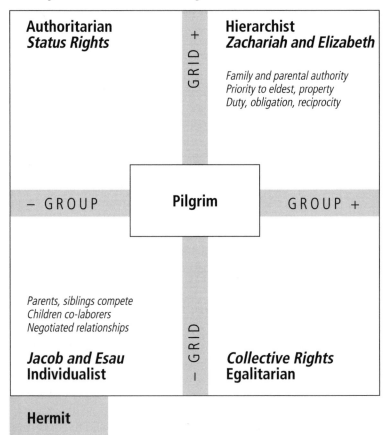

Domestic Authority

Most Christians assume that there is a biblical model for family relationships. The family game with which they are most familiar (their own) is the one that they believe is biblically based. When they read the Scriptures, they find proof-texts that support their analysis and conclude that any other form of family relationship is against biblical doctrine, yet the preceding data suggest a more complex picture.

Most of the extended case material on family in the Bible is found in the Old Testament. A careful analysis of this case material will show that the structure of family relations changes from one period of time to another and from case to case (see Lingenfelter 1996). The data presented in the New Testament are much more sparse, but again careful analysis suggests a diversity that one would expect from the model of prototype social games.

Anthropologists have engaged in extensive comparative study of family relationships over the course of the twentieth century. The outcome of this analysis demonstrates both a marvelous diversity and some distinctive but common patterns of relationship that are found in the structuring of families around the world. A classic work on this subject is George Peter Murdock's *Social Structure* (1949). Murdock identifies thirteen major types of kinship and family systems among the world's diverse cultures. While we will not explore the rich diversity of family systems, this chapter will show how significant values in family are linked inextricably to variables of the four prototype social games. I will argue that issues of authority in the family are shaped primarily by the preferred social game. Further, contrary to common opinion, the teachings of Scripture do not support one particular kind of authority as prescribed by a specific social game but rather call for transformation of authority relationships in any social environment into a pattern shaped more in the image of Christ.

The application of the model of prototype games to family units has some inherent limitations. First, family units tend to be the smallest and most variable units in society. As such they reflect the individuality and diversity of their members; no two families are exactly alike. Second, family structures vary significantly across cultures. Comparative research (Netting, Wilk, and Arnould 1984) has documented significant structural and functional variation that makes generalizations hazardous at best. The prototype game model has not been used by others as a tool for analysis of domestic units, and I proceed here with caution, acknowledging the tendency to oversimplify complex human behavior.

Let us begin with the subject of family relationships. In my American, middle-class, Christian context, we tend to think of family first in terms of the husband/wife relationship. This is a horizontal relationship of people in the same generation who establish their own household and live independently of others in the society. Many peoples of the world think of family more in terms of vertical generational relationships, referencing first the parent/child relationship and sometimes including grandparent or higher generations. This is evident in the cases of Jacob and Zachariah. The vertical focus is a necessary element of societies that value kinship groups and place authority in the hands of elder members of the group. The horizontal focus is possible where individuality is highly valued and accountability to others is restricted to role obligations or is negotiated personally.

The second factor of importance is the nature of domestic authority. My extended family and friends tend to think of authority in family relationships in terms of role definition and obligation. Father is head of the household, sometimes called Pop. Husband is provider even when both husband and wife produce incomes. Mother is the all-around utility person, "the cook, the cleaning lady, the driver, the nurse." Wife is both lover and maid. Other people in the world have a somewhat looser attitude about roles and domestic authority, focusing more on personal skill, interests, and relationships. The Deni Indians in Brazil, for example, occasionally switch sex roles; women go fishing while the men stay in the village, cook manioc, and care for the children. Such behavior would be scandalous in Yap, where it is forbidden for women to enter men's fishing waters.

Family authority relationships reflect the domestic organization of labor. This authority structure serves to organize production in family economic activities and provides the basis for the subsistence of the domestic group. The Yapese in Micronesia, for example, promote their sons to leadership only on the occasion of the death of the father and all of his younger brothers. The elder generation holds authority over the younger until all its members have died. This is reflected in the organization of domestic and communal labor; the elder generation of men gives the word and the younger generations run to do it. Domestic and community work groups are nearly always organized on the basis of peer relationships; each generation forms its peer work groups. When it is convenient to mobilize the extended family, the senior generation (male and female) takes the administrative role and the junior generations serve as laborers.

These case studies are by no means unique in human societies. The household in every society provides a foundational, organizational unit for the survival of the individual members. As such, a society lives or dies on the basis of the success of the organization of its domestic units.

The household serves not only for subsistence but also as the means of transmitting the material and cultural inheritance of the group. Children learn from their parents the basic means of production and the cultural values and standards by which people organize their activities with one another. The Deni Indian father teaches his son the skills of hunting, the value of self-sufficiency, and the independence of households by frequently realigning his own household with others and by releasing his son to a father-in-law to establish his own independent household. The American middle-class father emphasizes success in school, respect for property, and maintenance skills to manage a home and a career; the son gradually must earn money to cover his own expenses, leading to the establishment of an independent household. The domestic unit serves, then, to reproduce the primary structures and values of the social environment.

Because of the close connection between subsistence activities and the transmission of values and culture, one might expect societies and cultures to reproduce themselves without significant change in successive generations. Such a view is too simplistic, failing to recognize the dynamic characteristics of domestic units and social environments. In actuality, the members of any given family monitor the success or failure of their subsistence activities and use that feedback as information from which they learn and plan future activities. Success affirms domestic authority and activity, while failure usually provokes participants to reassess and sometimes to refocus or reorganize so as to meet their domestic needs. One of Jacob's sons, Joseph, learned the structure and social games of Egyptian culture and adapted effectively to them. We read in Genesis that when Joseph met his brothers on a much later occasion, he greeted them and interacted with them according to the values of the Egyptian world and culture rather than those of his own family unit. Seeing Joseph's success and their own failure during the famine, the whole family decided to follow Joseph into Egypt. After Jacob and his family settled there, they began a process of interaction with Egyptians, leading to new experience, feedback, and subsequent changes in their values, family structure, and social environment.

The household is crucial in every society because it provides the adaptive structure by which people survive and perpetuate themselves for succeeding generations. As members of these units find new ways of accomplishing these objectives, they will adjust their activities and ultimately their structures to accomplish this goal. They change their culture and adapt to their circumstances because they see change of direct relevance to their survival and to the perpetuation of their family.

Domestic Authority and Family Sins

Jewish family structure at the time of Christ is best characterized as a hierarchist social game. This type of family is neither unique to the Jewish people nor especially endorsed by Scripture. The features of Jewish family life described in the Gospels can be traced directly to the tribal and kingdom periods of Jewish society and culture. Similar family structures are typical of pagan cultures scattered widely throughout the Middle East, Africa, Asia, and around the world.

Following upon the presupposition stated in the first chapter, we shall consider each type of family structure in some way or another fallen and in conflict with the redeeming work of the Lord Jesus Christ. No family structure is God-given or biblically

endorsed; families are human institutions that may be transformed through the redemptive work of Christ.

The question then becomes not which of these family structures have a correct biblical frame but rather what sins are typical of each of these social games, thereby creating a need for the
redemptive work of Christ. Figure 6.2 details the distinctive sins
of parents and siblings that may commonly occur in each of the
four distinctive social games.

We need to reflect only briefly on the case study of Jacob to
identify sins typical of the individualist social game. The behavior of Rebekah, Jacob, Esau, Laban, Leah, and Rachel showed
something of an amoral familism practiced among these people. Their primary objectives were to advance self-interest and
their particular family interests in opposition to those of their
other relatives. They sacrificed principles for the sake of personal gain and did not hesitate to use deception and intrigue to
meet personal or family objectives. Jacob's attitude reflects the
ideal that doing for oneself is the primary goal, and his economic
practice suggests that the ends justify the means (bargaining for
his brother's birthright, stealing his brother's blessing, breeding
his father-in-law's flocks to produce for his own flocks).

Members of some evangelical, middle-class American families who embrace an authoritarian family game are quick to see
and criticize the behavior of Jacob, Rebekah, Rachel, and Laban.
However, to see the sins that typify their own social game is
much more difficult. For example, it is appropriate for authoritarian fathers to be disciplinarians, yet discipline may become
more important than love. In their attempt to make children
independent, they may fail to see how their strategies to create
separation and self-sufficiency often yield loneliness and isolation as well as independence. While teaching their children the
value of independent property and the necessity to care for their
own things, they may fail to see that they are also teaching that
self is more important than others and that self-interest is more
important than sharing with those in need. The emphasis on
good grades may press a child toward achievement at the
expense of honesty. Parents may also teach that the rule is more
important than the person.

The case studies of the prodigal son and David's family in the
Old Testament illustrate that parents and siblings of hierarchist

Figure 6.2
Sins of Parents in Four Social Games

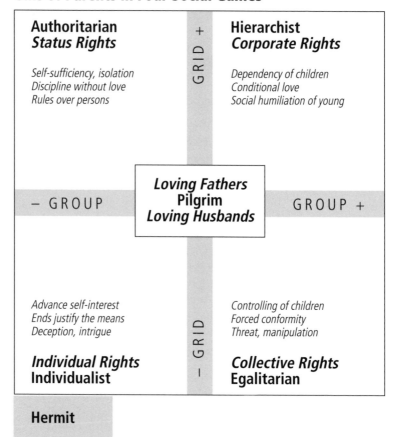

Authoritarian *Status Rights*	**Hierarchist** *Corporate Rights*
Self-sufficiency, isolation *Discipline without love* *Rules over persons*	*Dependency of children* *Conditional love* *Social humiliation of young*

GRID +

− GROUP

**Loving Fathers
Pilgrim
Loving Husbands**

GROUP +

GRID −

Advance self-interest *Ends justify the means* *Deception, intrigue*	*Controlling of children* *Forced conformity* *Threat, manipulation*
Individual Rights **Individualist**	***Collective Rights*** **Egalitarian**

Hermit

families also have their own unique sins. In these corporate family groups, property becomes exceedingly important to the members. Parents may typically use property to control their children. Jesus uses the parable of the prodigal son to perhaps refute the commonly held conception of a just father and to illustrate the will of his Father in heaven. The father forgives the son who dissipated his inheritance and restores him as a member of the family. This is highly uncharacteristic of hierarchist parental behavior. Parents in this type of social environment often hold their children in a lifelong dependency relationship, which may lead to immaturity and irresponsibility. David's sons are an unfortunate example. Hierarchist parents often extend conditional love in return for obedience and submission on the part of their children. The obedient son in Jesus' parable complains to his father because he had always been submissive and served his father, whereas the younger brother had been disobedient; the sibling's conclusion is that love for his wayward brother should be withdrawn and that he should be excluded from their family relations. Younger children may be humiliated by their older siblings and may be exploited for the good of corporate family interests. Finally, hierarchist parents and siblings often avoid showing tenderness and compassion; the criticism of the elder brother in the parable of the prodigal son stands over against his father's tenderness and compassion. Family authority and public reputation may be more important than tenderness and compassion in the hierarchist family.

The egalitarian social game often produces parents who seek total control over their children. Aukan parents threaten their children with random malicious acts of ancestral spirits if they fail to support the interest of the group. Nonconforming Aukan children are pressured socially and rubbed ritually (literally with herbal washes to purify them) until blended into or excluded from family relationships. This pattern of pressing for conformity is not unique to the Aukan. A Chinese proverb says that a nail that sticks out must be pounded until it is even with the rest of the surface. Aukan families pound and rub their members until they are like everyone else. Parents may manipulate their children in marriages and may force them to break up a marriage if it does not meet parental interests. The collective group seeks to control individuals for good or evil interests.

In conclusion, each social game has its own unique forms and expressions of oppression and sin in the relationships between parents and children. The sins of the parents and the sins of the siblings arise not only out of their private interests but also out of the social games in which they participate. The individualist and egalitarian social games produce sins of excess in which either the individual or the group manipulates others to achieve selfish ends. In authoritarian and hierarchist games, where rule has much greater priority over social behavior, legalism and the abuse of authority are much more common. People use law and authority against others rather than for just and compassionate ends.

Biblical Metaphors, Domestic Authority, and Pilgrimage

How does the gospel challenge each of these family games? In what ways are family members called to be transforming agents within their social environments? To what extent does Scripture address their specific sins? What are the biblical metaphors of family relationships that help us refocus our priorities to Christian pilgrimage?

The story of the prodigal son illustrates how Jesus addressed the sins of the hierarchist social game. The righteous father treasures his sons more than his property. When his younger son requested his share of the inheritance, the father released that inheritance rather than hold his son in a dependency relationship to him. The father loved this son unconditionally, accepting him back even when he had dissipated all of his inheritance and lived a life of utter disgrace to the family. The father rebuked the elder brother when he complained about his father's compassion and celebration for the younger. At the same time, the father did not betray his elder son by dividing the property again. The younger had lost his property, and the consequences of that act remained. Forgiveness entailed restoration of relationship in the family and provision of food and clothing but not a restocking of his former wealth.

The metaphor that is taught so profoundly in this parable and repeated throughout the New Testament is that of the loving father. "For God so loved the world" (John 3:16); "God demonstrates his own love for us in this: While we were still sinners, Christ died for us" (Rom. 5:8); "how great is the love the Father has lavished on us" (1 John 3:1). The metaphor of the loving father not only is appropriate for this hierarchist family but also can be expressed in unique and appropriate ways in each of the four games. One might ask the reader to recreate the story of the prodigal son in each of the other three social games. What would the son seek in each of the other three family types? How would the elder brother respond? How might the father manifest the love of God and deal with two sinning sons as Jesus did in his parable?

A second major theme that we see in the Scriptures is love of God and of one's neighbor (Deut. 6:5–6; Matt. 22:38–39). Loving one's neighbor as oneself takes different forms in each of the four social games. Jacob and Esau would have behaved differently if they had practiced this principle of loving each other as they loved themselves. American siblings who do not have contact with one another for years would make a greater effort to keep contact and support one another if they practiced this principle. Yapese parents and siblings would be able to show more tenderness and compassion for one another and forgive the unsubmissive and the disobedient. The Aukan and the Chinese would not be so insistent upon pounding in the nail that sticks up or rubbing to exclusion their family members who find it difficult to fit in.

A third metaphor repeated in several places in the New Testament is that of the loving husband. Ephesians 5:25 challenges husbands to "love your wives, just as Christ loved the church and gave himself up for her." This metaphor carried special power for Paul's Greek readers, whose families typically arranged their marriages without regard to the opinions of the young people involved. Fathers used their children to create advantageous alliances for their families, with the result that most husbands had little affection for their wives and women had little respect for husbands who did not love them. Paul, who was not married, calls for radical transformation in husband/wife relationships. Peter, perhaps a married realist, tells believing husbands to "be considerate" and to treat their wives "with respect as the weaker partner and as heirs with you of the gracious gift of life" (1 Peter 3:7).

Psychologists tell us that many family problems are generated from the strained and broken relationships between father and mother in a family unit. How a man expresses love as a husband will vary in each social environment. Yet, in my experience observing families in diverse parts of the world and in each of these social games, I have seen loving husbands who have fulfilled these New Testament commands within the context of their own culture and social environment. A loving husband can be a transforming power in family and society. If Jacob had treated Leah with the same respect and love that he gave to Rachel, the conflicts between these two women could have been largely resolved, which in turn would have had a transforming power upon their children.

Finally, the Scriptures challenge women to be wives worthy of respect (1 Tim. 3:11). In each of the social games, authority is allocated in a particular way within the family unit. In some social games the husband and father has more exclusive authority than in other social environments. It is, however, true in every social game that husbands and wives share authority within the family in socially prescribed ways, and husbands and fathers always have some interest and authority in relationship to their children. The biblical writers encourage and admonish wives to submit to their husbands (Eph. 5:22; Col. 3:18). Families cannot operate effectively without the allocation of authority among the members. The Scriptures promise that women who live worthy of respect and who are submissive to their husbands in their particular social environment will have a transforming power and influence in society. Peter says, "They [unbelieving husbands] may be won over without words by the behavior of their wives, when they see the purity and reverence of your lives" (1 Peter 3:1–2).

To sum up, the diverse and varied forms of family found around the world are part of the creative genius of human life and culture. The Scriptures do not prescribe a single family form or a single social game by which people may be identified as followers of Christ. Rather, the metaphors of the gospel call for transformed relationships between husbands and wives and parents and children within the social environments and domestic groups of culture. The commands given to us in Old and New Testament alike lead us to transformed relationships and domestic groups that have a powerful transforming impact on the society at large.

Christian Pilgrimage for Aukan Believers

Louis Shanks (1987, 14–16) describes the marriage of a man named Da Sonobi in the village of Manlobi. Da Sonobi was reared in his mother's home, and his marriage was arranged by his lineage-father (mother's elder brother) rather than his father. Da Sonobi's first wife came from a different clan and lineage but lived in the same village. After they were married, Da Sonobi moved to his wife's lineage and built a house for her there; at times he returned to his own lineage and stayed in his deceased lineage-father's house.

Some time after his marriage, Da Sonobi had an incestuous relationship with a girl in his own clan, which created an uproar in the village. In punishment for this violation of the incest taboo, he was beaten by village priests at the mortuary in an attempt to appease the ancestress spirits. He was then banished to another village. A girl was born from this taboo union, but she died (as people expected) when she was about three years old.

Da Sonobi's affair created tension with his wife, and they were separated. He then married a woman from the village of Keementi and lived there until the storm over the incestuous relationship had died. As Da Sonobi grew older he took another wife, this time closer to home in the adjacent village of Fandaaki. Taking up residence with this woman allowed him to resume a role in his lineage of birth where gradually over many years he became a leader. During these years he traveled back and forth between his two wives, spending time with each, and with the men in their villages, until they died. Finally, as an old man of more than seventy years, he married a third woman from the village of Tabiki. While he spent some time in her village, they lived most of their time in Manlobi, residing in Da Sonobi's lineage where he was an elder and village leader.

The basic theme running through this book is that all peoples are in their prison of disobedience and the gospel will bring conflict and change into the lives of each and every group. The gospel creates significant conflict for Aukan believers in their marriages and family customs. Malachi 2:16 states clearly that God hates divorce. Jesus speaks openly against divorce (Matt. 5:31–32; Luke 16:18). Paul repeats a similar message in his letter to the Corinthians (1 Cor. 7). The sanctity of marriage is attributed to the created order (Gen. 2:24; Mark 10:6–9). While the issue of multiple marriages is more complex, since they were obviously permitted in early Hebrew history, the epistles state clearly that church leaders have only one wife.

Some people may question the Aukan practice of granting a maternal uncle more authority for the instruction of a child than is given to the father. While at first glance this seems unusual and inconsistent with some biblical texts (see Prov. 13:24; 19:18; Eph. 6:4), parental authority is a more important issue than the specific role of the father. In fact, Aukan people separate the role of nurture and care from the role of authority and instruction. The biological father is the one who provides nurture and care for the child, while the maternal uncle, serving as lineage-father, exercises authority and instructs the child in appropriate social behavior. One might argue that it is easier for Aukan men to hear, understand, and receive the message of God as the loving Father than it is for many men in Western societies who have been reared in homes where fathers are harsh, distant authoritarian figures who show little if any love and affection for their sons. Aukan men are much more receptive to the gospel than are Aukan women.

The strong Aukan emphasis on brother and sister relationships is sustained in the Gospels (Matt. 23:8; Mark 3:35; John 21:23) and the epistles (Rom. 8:29; Heb. 2:11). The Scriptures also support the Aukan belief that women exerting authority over men is bad. Aukan men find comfort in biblical passages that admonish women to submit to their husbands in the Lord, since the collective power of women in Aukan villages can be abusive and destructive to men.

The case study of Asoinda, a believer in the neighboring Saramaccan society, illustrates the power of women in these societies. When Asoinda accepted the message of the gospel and proclaimed publicly his faith in the Lord Jesus Christ, all three of his Saramaccan wives rejected him. They refused to receive him into their homes and provoked their fellow villagers to reject him from the village, keeping him from seeing his children. Asoinda became an outcast in his own village. All of his wives divorced him and remarried. Since these women and their brothers control the children, Asoinda has had almost no contact with them since his conversion.

For more than ten years Asoinda has dedicated himself to evangelism, teaching new believers, and working to translate the Scriptures into his mother tongue. He has rejoiced in his opportunity to suffer for the gospel's sake, giving up wives and children, brothers and sisters as Jesus proclaimed in Luke 14:26. He is praying that God might one day give him a Christian wife and children who know the Lord and follow his leadership.

The Aukan and Saramaccan converts recognize that a new set of brothers and sisters in Christ supersede their clan and lineage ties. In their churches in the city of Paramaribo, these believers have formed a new clan, the local church. The elder men and women work together to teach the younger men, women, and children the words of Scripture and the rules for life that come from being followers of Jesus Christ. Men and women still look to their elder brothers and sisters for help in training their children in the Lord. Christian families emphasize the authority of the senior generation and relationships of brothers and sisters more than they emphasize the authority of father over child or the authority of husband over wife. At the same time Christian Aukan men and women have committed themselves to one husband and one wife, to a lifelong marriage in Christ, and to the rule of elders in their family and in their church relationships.

Christian Pilgrimage for Yapese Believers

During a conversation in 1970 with an old Yapese man, Tamag, and his wife, Rungun, she began to complain about her son's wife. She said the girl was frivolous and lazy. All she ever did was comb her hair, make sweet-smelling garlands, and drive around in her husband's car. Rungun began to complain that Yapese girls were not learning the proper way of life. Most of them did not know anything about gardening or preparing food. How could they ever have children and take care of them the way a Yapese woman should?

At this point, Tamag interrupted and said that he had been like his son when he was a young man. He liked beautiful girls. He even married a few of those girls, but he did not stay married very long. Then, as he got older, he began to realize that he needed a hard-working wife to take care of his need for food and to bear heirs for his estate. He began to look around for the right kind of woman who could provide for him in his old age. He explained that this was the reason he married Rungun.

Rungun nodded her head with approval and then elaborated further on the ideal Yapese woman. A woman should go to her taro garden early every morning to weed, plant, cultivate, and obtain food for that day. She should have fresh food daily for her husband and children, and if there are leftovers, she should eat them herself.

Yapese describe marriage as something of a contest of exchanges between a man and a woman. A man's contribution entails land, names for the children, resources, and labor. Land and names are fundamental to life. A Yapese lacking an ancestral name has no right to inherit the lands of his father. In addition to these, a man provides the heavy labor for clearing gardens. A man's primary work, however, is on the sea. When Yapese sit down to a meal, they must have both vegetable foods and fish. If one element is lacking, someone has not kept part of the reciprocal obligation.

Rungun concluded that a good wife should be submissive to her husband and to her mother-in-law. She said her son's wife was lazy and unresponsive. When Rungun asked the girl to come along to work, she always had an excuse and ran away. If Rungun had her way, she would send that girl back to her family and arrange another marriage for her son. She had in mind a girl who already had her own productive taro and yam gardens on land given to her by her mother. Any girl who drove around in a car and never stayed home could not be good. She was probably flirting with other men when she should be working with her mother-in-law in her gardens.

Marital conflict is common on Yap, in spite of the fact the young people marry for love. Marital conflict and divorce are most frequently precipitated by affairs. If a couple has been married for a short time and have no children, an affair will probably end the marriage abruptly. The woman will take her personal belongings and return to her father's household. If the couple has children, the matter becomes more serious. The husband may beat an unfaithful wife severely until she reforms her ways. A wife, however, has less power over an unfaithful husband. She may first harangue him publicly to shame him for his behavior. If this is unsuccessful, she may refuse to cook for him or to perform other domestic services. Most Yapese have made three or more attempts to find a successful marriage.

Perhaps our best insight into the transforming significance of the gospel for Yapese marriage comes from a Yapese believer. In 1980 I interviewed an old man by the name of Fiithingmew, who because of diabetes had lost one of his legs. His father had been something of a scholar of Yapese culture and had passed on that gift and interest to Fiithingmew. As a believer, confined to his house for most of his days or moving about on crutches, he had become a student of Scripture. He accepted the Scriptures as the source of authority and truth, yet he had the unique ability to reflect on his culture and discover analogies that provided a clearer understanding of Scripture.

In our conversation, Fiithingmew said that the Yapese word for marriage, *mabgol*, had hidden meanings that cast light upon the relationship of a Christian husband and wife and upon the relationship of a believer with God. Part of the word for marriage, *mab*, is the Yapese word for "door." The Yapese may use the word as either a noun or a verb. To say *ka mab* is to say, "It's open." The second part of the word for marriage, *gol*, is the word for "generosity." A *bagol* gives to others whatever is asked and more abundantly than has been requested. Yapese honor men and women for their generosity. To be called *bagol* is to be recognized as possessing one of the finest character traits that one can have in Yap.

Fiithingmew said that the ideal marriage is one characterized by *mabgol*, "open generosity." He said that a Christian husband and wife should be completely open to one another, withholding nothing, giving whatever is asked and more. A man and a woman should share without reservation their labor, their material goods, their love, and their respect. Giving should be without consideration of return, and a marriage partner should seek to give more than the other could ever return.

Fiithingmew likened this to Paul's instructions to believers in Ephesians 5. He noted how Paul commanded wives to submit to their husbands and husbands to love their wives as Christ loved the church. He said that Christ's love for the church was *mabgol*. Christ withheld nothing of himself from the church; he gave himself to his disciples and to the people he taught and healed during his ministry on earth. He laid down his life on the cross for all who would believe.

Fiithingmew suggested that even now Christ extends to us, through his relationship with the Father in heaven, open generosity. God has promised to show the incomparable riches of his grace and to provide all of our needs according to his riches in glory (Phil. 4:19) through Christ. He noted that we believers, members of his church, as the bride of Christ have a marriage partnership with Christ. We are to give him whatever is asked. All of the good gifts that we have—our labor, our goods, our thanksgiving, our love, our respect—we should return to Christ, just as he has extended to us all that is available to him in his relationship with the Father.

I came away from this conversation with Fiithingmew deeply touched by his understanding of the Scripture and by the analogy of Yapese marriage to the relationship between Christ and the church. As he articulated his thoughts, it became clear to me that I could learn much from the concept of *mabgol*, not only for my relationship with Christ but also for my relationship to my own wife. The wonder of the gospel is that it redeems not only people but also their creativity, enabling them to articulate their understanding of their relationship with God and to create distinctive and unique avenues of communication of truth. Through these creative insights, believers from distinctive cultures may help one another, as members in the body of Christ, to comprehend the joy of deeper relationship with God and redeemed relationships with members of family and society.

7

Authority and Community
The Context of Local Churches

Case Studies

The Javanese Pastor

A large population of Indonesian Javanese came a century ago as immigrants to work on Surinam plantations. Many of these people stayed after their labor term was completed, and in 1986 they formed a population of around sixty thousand. Living in and around the city of Paramaribo, they for the most part practiced the Islamic faith blended with Javanese animism. In the 1980s many responded to a significant movement of the Spirit of God, and the Javanese evangelical church grew rapidly.

One young pastor stands out in the church movement among the Surinam Javanese. This man became a believer in the early 1970s and, under the discipleship of a missionary, studied the Scriptures and committed his life to preaching the gospel to the Javanese. His success as an evangelist and a church planter was recounted in chapter 1. He also served as the primary mother-tongue translator for the Surinam Javanese language.

As the church grew and the pastor's responsibilities became increasingly demanding, his Bible translation associates began encouraging him to delegate some of his responsibilities to younger men whom he had been discipling. They were concerned because the work of Bible translation had nearly ceased. After some months the pastor recruited another man to help him in the translation program, but he refused to allow this young man to do any translating of Scripture, limiting him to transcribing old Surinam Javanese stories. A frustrated translation team encouraged the pastor to release some of his trainees to carry on the Javanese work, arguing that he had many capable men working under him. They pointed to several lay leaders whom he had been discipling and encouraged him to allow them to take more responsibility for the total church work. They suggested that a co-worker with the Bible translation organization might begin translation drafts that he then could revise at a later time.

The pastor resolutely refused to follow their counsel, explaining that these men were not ready yet to carry on the work of the ministry. Citing their lack of experience and training, he refused to give responsibility to them until he was confident that they were truly qualified. The translation team argued that the men would grow and mature. Further, the amount of work to be done was so great, more workers were needed. Even immature men could help to carry more of the load.

The disagreement that ensued between the missionary leaders and pastor, while not one of open conflict, created tension and frustration. The missionaries, who were financially supporting the translation work, were discouraged at the rate of progress. At the same time they were positive and excited about the growth in the Javanese church and were stymied as to exactly how to proceed without retarding that growth. To them, the pastor held the key, if only he would release more of his leaders to carry on the work of the church while he concentrated on the Bible translation work. The pastor, unwilling to release his workers, delegated to them a limited amount of authority. These men carried out their responsibilities effectively. The pastor's presence and leadership assured strict control over the total church activities, building a community that was rich in its depth and responsive in every way to the needs and concerns of its members. The pastor's lay leaders held an intense, deep loyalty to him and submitted readily to his leadership, following him in the work of the church. Likewise, the members of the church expressed open and affectionate loyalty to him; the group was very strong in its corporate and worship activities. One of the most appealing aspects of the church to new believers was the strength of the community and its genuine warmth and love for them as they entered it.

The tension between mission and church leaders arose from their conflicting expectations regarding work productivity and their rules of authority and responsibility for leaders and supporting workers. They had contrary solutions on how to manage an increasing work load.

The Aukan Pastors

In the chapter on labor (chap. 4) we considered the case of a Bible translation team seeking the support of Aukan pastors for two young Aukan mother-tongue translators. The team asked an association of Aukan churches in Paramaribo to provide partial support for the salaries of these mother-tongue translators. The pastors and elders of these churches resisted the missionary proposal. They complained that the young men who were working for the translation organization were unproved as leaders. They said that they had not worked for or contributed to the continuing ministries of the local congregations.

As the translation team explored the opposition to these young men they discovered that the pastors themselves were not paid by members of their congregations. Only the senior pastor in the First Church in Paramaribo earned a salary. All of the other pastors gained their income through full-time jobs in other sectors. Further, the pastors and elders in these congregations began their service as young men, working for the Lord in any task given to them by the elders. Over many years their congregations and elders had rewarded their faithfulness with increased responsibility in the church. They serve as pastors and elders because of their previous faithful service to their congregations.

These pastors and elders saw these younger men, chosen by missionaries for the task of Bible translation, as only casually interested in the ministry of the church and primarily interested in gaining a salary. They recognized that these young men were educated, multilingual, and able to do the translation work. However, they did not see them as committed members of the church who were spiritually worthy of the work of translation. Further, comparing their own ministries to that of these younger men, they asked why these men could not contribute their time for Bible translation as they contributed time for church ministry. The Aukan pastors and elders refused to support the translation project and questioned the legitimacy of the young men chosen by the mission to do the work.

Authority and Power

To understand authority it is useful to focus specifically on the issue of power. In every society the question of authority resides ultimately in the distribution of power between individuals and between individuals and groups. In the preceding case study, the Aukan pastors and elders did not have power apart from their church members to make decisions about the use of offerings and the support of the Bible translation project. The Javanese pastor, in contrast, had a great deal of power over his congregation and co-workers and refused to relinquish it to others who were working under him.

The Aukan pastors and elders play an egalitarian social game in which the leaders have limited power over others. Church members allocate power to their elders on the record of their faithful service and may readily withdraw that power if and when the pastor or an elder fails to serve them. Members of Aukan churches hold high standards for participation in the church community, and the leaders are the exemplars of those standards. People who are less committed may attend their services but may not participate in the inner core of the congregation or take leadership responsibility.

Linkages in Aukan churches are primarily based upon strong ties of faith, fellowship, and service. Members also are often linked by kinship, marriage, and reciprocity. Pastors, elders, and members seek to serve one another in the urban community by helping families in need, educating children in the Lord, and caring for those who are sick or destitute. The local church calendar is filled with times of worship, celebration, Bible study, evangelism, and service ministries to members and their families that are led by these unpaid, voluntary pastors and elders.

The Surinam Javanese differentiate relationships within and outside the church in a hierarchist social game. The Christians who have joined the Paramaribo congregation have allocated power to the pastor and allow him to speak for them and make decisions on their behalf. The pastor in turn has delegated power to some of his lay leaders, who then conduct different aspects of the ministry under him.

The members of the city church do not live in coordinated village or neighborhood settings. While some live in villages in surrounding districts, most are residents of the metropolitan area of the city of Paramaribo and live in scattered Javanese neighborhoods. Their relationship as a group has little to do with residential proximity but rather is generated from their commitment as new believers to the Surinam Javanese congregation. Organized activities encourage unity and fellowship in the group. The most important activity is a regionwide service held every Saturday evening. This is a service of celebration, worship, and fellowship rather than a service of teaching. During this time people gather from all over Paramaribo and spend the evening together, enjoying each other's company and celebrating their unity in Christ. On other days members gather in four distinctive areas for Bible study, prayer, and small-group fellowship. Bible studies are also social times in which people eat together and work together for their fellowship in Christ. The pastor tries to be at all of these, guiding lay leaders to shepherd these small-group fellowships. On Sunday afternoons large-group activities, such as baptisms, soccer games, or other events, bring people together for fun and fellowship. Coordination among the Surinam Javanese is based upon social and worship activities rather than geographic proximity. These activities create the links between people that emphasize group participation and group membership. The pastor has made a considered effort to celebrate the collective joy of Christians and the fellowship that people have together in the church of Christ; their meetings create a sense of joy, celebration, and unity as he disciples them and trains them in the Scripture.

Authority and Community

Power authority is the legitimate right, held by a social elite, to control people and/or resources in a given social setting (Adams 1975). An individual may gain power authority by the mere ownership of significant resources or by controlling the access of others to those resources. When resources are held or controlled by individuals independently of others, they have independent power. Power authority may also be allocated by a group of people to their leaders (Aukan and Javanese cases), who then act on their behalf; having gained authority by consensus or majority support from members of the group, these leaders have allocated power. Power authority may also be delegated by leaders to subordinates; these subordinate leaders hold delegated power, often legitimized by an institutional structure, in which the locus of power is held by leaders at the top.

Skill authority refers to control of information or technology derived from the mastery of particular technical skills and occupying a role assigned to people who hold such skills. Teachers have particular skill authority related to the subject matter that they have studied at great length. Mechanics have skill authority based upon their ability to repair automobiles or other kinds of machinery. Individuals who hold skills, such as carpenters, plumbers, dentists, chemists, and computer technicians, have authority that derives from their mastery of that skill and is based upon the needs of others in their society for their expertise.

Figure 7.1 illustrates how power and skill authority are elaborated and applied for community leadership in four distinctive social games. In the high grid social games, power authority is elaborated and expressed in all of its forms. In the hierarchist game, the corporate interests of the group place significant constraints upon leaders. Seniority may have greater value than skill, although specialization is important for the selection and legitimacy of leaders. Leaders have limited independent authority; group dialogue and corporate accountability dominate the decision process. Authority is allocated by the group, leaders hold specific titles, and authority is elaborated in specific role expectations for group members. In the authoritarian social game, the top leaders have independent power and exercise significantly greater control over subordinate roles through delegated authority. Skill authority is a primary factor in role differentiation, and skilled leaders play significant roles in administrative structures.

Figure 7.1
Social Games and Community Authority

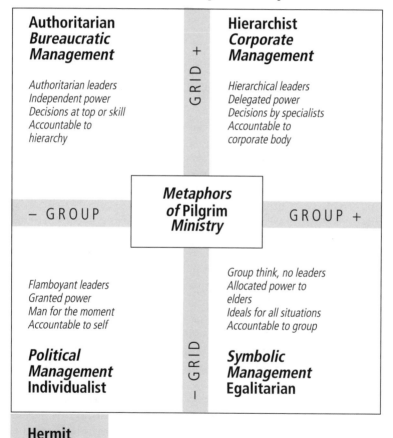

Authoritarian
Bureaucratic
Management

Authoritarian leaders
Independent power
Decisions at top or skill
Accountable to
hierarchy

Hierarchist
Corporate
Management

Hierarchical leaders
Delegated power
Decisions by specialists
Accountable to
corporate body

GRID +

– GROUP

Metaphors
of Pilgrim
Ministry

GROUP +

Flamboyant leaders
Granted power
Man for the moment
Accountable to self

Political
Management
Individualist

Group think, no leaders
Allocated power to
elders
Ideals for all situations
Accountable to group

Symbolic
Management
Egalitarian

– GRID

Hermit

In low grid social environments power authority is limited to the reciprocal granting of power between individuals and the allocation of power from a group to its collective elders. Skill authority confers little more than prestige and personal advantage to those who have it. In the individualist social game individuals grant power reciprocally, but no further elaboration occurs. Individuals play out personal dramatic roles in the life and work of the community, to the admiration or scorn of others around them. Skill confers prestige but not authority over others. In the egalitarian social game, members of the group allocate authority to either elders or skilled members but retain strict control over them through the demands of consensus. Positions and privileges of authority are few and unelaborated, and an ethos of egalitarianism pervades group life.

Mission and National Conflicts

The Javanese Pastor: Corporate or Bureaucratic Decisions?

The chapter opened with a case study of the Surinam Javanese pastor in conflict with his Bible translation co-workers. The pastor's missionary colleagues questioned his leadership, suggesting that he was unwilling to delegate tasks to capable subordinates. While the mission team's conclusion was correct, I believe that a partial explanation of the conflict rests in their distinctive social games, with the added complication of the pastor's personality type. The mission team operates from a weak authoritarian social game, in which task orientation and skill authority are the primary basis for organizing work. The Javanese church, in contrast, employs a hierarchist game in which the pastor holds power allocated by the members of his congregation, with strong emphasis on seniority and competence. The Javanese pastor believes that the unity of his group depends very much upon the loyalty of the people to him, as well as to one another, and he therefore delegates authority with great caution. As new converts who for the most part did not have extensive social ties before they joined as believers, their relationships formed around a nucleus of fellowship activities and pastoral leadership.

The corporate solidarity of the new church grows out of expectations spawned in the villages and neighborhoods from which most of the members originate. Outside of the city, villagers see themselves as a corporate group, with a high degree of commitment to one another. The whole village attends a funeral. To build a house, the men gather to work and the women prepare food to feed them. Families share food from their respective gardens, mutual labor, and support at births, marriages, and other key family events. Village Javanese emphasize harmony, togetherness, and commitment to group goals.

Members of the city church struggle with the tensions created by their conversion to Christianity. By the mere fact that they live in the city, they have broken from the corporate villages of their childhood. Yet family and village ties remain as strong pulls upon them. Acceptance of the Christian faith has created further strains with family members, and some have been ostracized for their public baptism and proclamation of faith. The church provides a new corporate community, a new group of kin with whom they may express harmony, loyalty, and mutual support.

The pastor, taking the power allocated to him by these people, has built community through the many celebrations and social and spiritual events that are part of their worship and fellowship. At the same time, he is careful not to delegate too much power to individuals who represent segments of the larger group. These younger men, who are his disciples, are not in his estimation ready to take over the major responsibilities of either Bible translation or pastoral leadership. A perfectionist in personality, he retains tight authority over the whole and carefully supervises the work of each of these individuals. The corporate values and needs of these Christian converts are well served as he oversees a tightly knit church community, united through his personal and corporate leadership.

Whereas the pastor is preoccupied with the corporate unity of the church, training the persons who work under him and nurturing them to assume positions of leadership, his mission colleagues are task-oriented and concerned about getting the job of translation done on a time schedule that they themselves have determined. These different presuppositions have led to tension between the pastor and his mission colleagues. They

work from an expert/trainee model, whereas he operates on the
basis of a senior pastor/junior lay leader framework. The
elder/younger dichotomy in Surinam Javanese culture sustains
the pastor's leadership. He holds authority, and the younger men
serve in positions of prolonged subordination to his leadership
and control. The mission team, in contrast, working from the
expert/trainee model, sees the training as just a matter of time.
Once the training is completed, the individual should be released
to do the job. Training in the bureaucratic system takes a limited period of time, after which the student assumes a role at
least of some equality with the master teacher. These differences
and the personalities involved produced a stalemate in the translation project. The mission team wonders whether or not the
pastor will relinquish authority in the longer term when his disciples are more mature.

Aukan Translators: Technically Qualified versus Corporately Qualified

The conflict between the Aukan translation team and the local
pastors and elders is more clearly focused upon very different
social games and assumptions about authority. The mission
team employed two young Aukan men because of their education and linguistic skills and expected that local churches would
be willing to help support them for the contribution they were
making to the future of Aukan churches. The team had specific
technical requirements for the job, and these young men seemed
well qualified. They adopted a bureaucratic variant of the
authoritarian game to organize the translation project.

The pastors, in contrast, saw these young men as part of their
congregations and as part of a larger group of people (egalitarian social game) who were participating in a total ministry.
Since only the most senior of the pastors received a salary, to
pay these young men for church work seemed totally out of line.
Furthermore, they believed the mission organization should
pay these men on the same basis that the government paid people for labor. If the church were to support such projects, they
would do so only after the young men had earned their trust
and support. All of the leaders in the church had received their
assignments because of their faithfulness and long-term (ten-

year or more) commitment to the group. These young men had not demonstrated either faithfulness or long-term commitment and were therefore not qualified for the support of the church community.

The misunderstanding between the mission team and the Aukan leaders grows from distinctive social games and expectations regarding authority. The mission team operates from bureaucratic authoritarian game social assumptions, whereas the Aukan church operates from egalitarian assumptions. For the Aukan technical qualifications carry little weight, whereas technical skills are mandatory for translation work. The mission felt that the Aukan church should support the translation project because it was for their benefit; the Aukan measured benefit primarily in terms of evidence of commitment to group goals.

The more important question for the Aukan translation team is not the financial support for the project but rather the legitimacy of the translation itself. If these technically qualified young men effectively translate the Scriptures into the Aukan language but are not accepted as spiritually mature members of their churches, then how will their work be accepted? The legitimacy of the final translated Scripture is inextricably intertwined with the character and commitment of these two men to their local churches. The most important priority for the translation project is not gaining partial salary support for these men but rather helping them become effective servants in the ministries of their local church. The only standard by which their work will be assessed is that by which the congregation and elders measure themselves.

But Doesn't the Bible Say . . . ?

When I have presented this material to seminary students or in workshops with missionaries in the field, someone inevitably raises the question, But doesn't the Bible say some very specific things about leadership and the church? My response to this is, Certainly. The Bible says very much about leaders, about the church, and about authority. The question is, What does the Bible say about leaders and authority? Should churches be organized according to a scriptural model, and if so what is it? Is there a correct structure taught in the Scriptures?

The first important fact for us to understand is that the church is always founded in an existing social context. The church in Jerusalem grew up in the midst of rabbinical Judaism and as such reflected much of its social context. The churches in Antioch, Ephesus, Corinth, and Rome were established in very different social and religious contexts from that in Jerusalem. It is evident as we read the letters of Paul that each of these social and religious contexts exerted significant pressure on these newly founded churches. Paul's discussion in Romans of the plan of God for Gentiles and Jews concludes that "God has bound all men over to disobedience so that he may have mercy on them all" (Rom. 11:32). Paul then admonishes the Roman Christians not to "conform any longer to the pattern of this world" (Rom. 12:2). What does it mean to not conform? If we are not to follow the pattern of the world, is there a pattern we are to follow? Is that pattern elaborated in the Scriptures?

If we can interpret Paul's comment universally, then Christians are to be not conformed to any and all of the social games that we find in the world. From the evidence presented thus far, it should be clear to the reader that a social environment exerts significant pressure on individuals in any given society. Individuals are pressed by people around them to conform to the values and relationships of the approved game in that social setting. From the cases that we have just examined it is evident that both missionary and national operate in conformity with their own social games. Their frustrations with one another grow out of their inability to break out of their social games. They are unable to accept the values and patterns of the other social games they encounter where they work. Conflicts between missionaries and nationals arise because each brings to their relationship values and authority expectations that arise from the context in which they have lived for much of their lives. In spite of Paul's pleas that Christians should not be conformed to the pattern of this world, Christian leaders, missionary and national alike, have difficulty thinking about relationships in any other terms.

What does the Bible say about social games? First, Scripture focuses not on factors of social environment but rather on the motives and actions of people within social environments. Jesus illustrates this most graphically in his dialogue with the Pharisees about their customary eating habits (Luke 14). Noting that the guests picked the places of honor at the table, Jesus did not criticize them for having high and low places but rather criticized their motives to obtain public honor. He did not criticize his host for having friends, relatives, and rich neighbors over to dinner but tells him that in so doing, he has already achieved his social reward. Jesus did not criticize the hierarchist social game but rather challenged these Jews to live within that context in a unique and different way, having a humble attitude and compassion for the helpless at the bottom of the society. Finally, he told them a story. "A certain man was preparing a great banquet and invited many guests" (Luke 14:16). The story creates a powerful metaphor, showing how the kingdom of God, where the honored guests are the "poor, the crippled, the blind and the lame," contrasts with the kingdoms of men.

Yet within this wider context of the message, Jesus and the apostles taught their disciples to submit, as part of the Christian pilgrimage, to the existing authorities. Jesus commanded his disciples to pay taxes to Caesar, and he himself submitted to the authority of the chief priest and the governor, Pontius Pilate. Paul commands Christians to submit to governing authorities (Rom. 13:1) and to pray for all secular authority (1 Tim. 2:2).

Metaphors of Ministry

What does the Bible say about leaders and authority? David W. Bennett (1993) notes that the terms *leader* and *leadership* do not appear in the Gospels. Rather, the profound emphasis in these texts is on following rather than leading. The metaphors of ministry that Jesus used to describe his followers, such as "witness," "servant," "salt," and "disciples," expand our understanding of the nature of leadership in the Christian church. Jesus clearly stated that his kingdom was not of this world, that his disciples were in the world but not of it. He called his disciples out of their social environment and, after an extended period of training, sent them back into it to live as pilgrims and strangers and to be salt and light.

From the references to authority in the Gospels it is clear that Jesus claimed special authority from the Father. The Jews noted that he taught as one having authority, and he proclaimed himself to have the authority to forgive sins and to cast out demons and unclean spirits. In Matthew 28:18 Jesus proclaims that "all authority in heaven and in earth has been given to me." Paul picks up the same theme in Ephesians 1:21 and Colossians 2:10, proclaiming Christ head over every authority and power.

Independent power in the church belongs exclusively to the Lord Jesus Christ. The apostles had no power of their own, but only that delegated to them by the Lord himself. Jesus gave the Twelve authority to drive out evil spirits, to heal disease and sickness, and to make disciples and teach. The Lord appeared directly to Saul and then through a messenger, Ananias, commanding him to carry his name before the Gentiles and their kings and before the people of Israel. Paul declares that his authority as an apostle comes directly from Jesus Christ (Gal. 1:1). The leadership of the apostles in the church is thus characterized as "followership," men who have been touched directly by the Lord Jesus Christ, who have been called to follow him, and who have received delegated authority to lead others to become followers of Jesus.

The Gospels record the process by which Jesus discipled the Twelve as apostles in training, and the Book of Acts documents how these apostles provided leadership for the early church. The sense of delegated authority, evidenced by the filling of the Holy Spirit (Acts 2:4; 6:8; 10:47) and witnessing of the fact of the resurrection of Christ in fulfillment of the Scriptures (Acts 1:4; 2:32; 5:29–32), pervades the Book of Acts. The apostles, Christ's emissaries, taught new believers and further delegated authority in the growing church to mature believers, "full of the Spirit and wisdom" (Acts 6:3), to serve the leadership needs of the local fellowship.

The delegated authority for church leaders in Acts 6 was derived from their relationship with Christ, the Holy Spirit, the Scriptures, and the apostles. The congregation selected and the apostles anointed mature men, filled with the Holy Spirit and wisdom (Acts 6:3, 6), to carry out the work of overseeing the distribution of food. The source of delegated authority in the church is universal and constitutes a kingdom principle for leadership in the universal church, but the process employed to confer that authority grows out of the social environment. In Acts 6 the church suffered growing pains, and the egalitarian organization was unable to cope with the strain. The congregation selected among its members and allocated authority to them, a routine social process and the only legitimate way in that social context to select new leaders.

Should churches be organized according to a scriptural model, and if so, what is it? Is there a correct structure of authority taught in the Scriptures? Many books have been written on this subject, and it would be naive to think that we could address this issue in a substantive way in a few short paragraphs. Many of the arguments for church structure and authority come from texts in the Book of Acts and in the Pastoral Epistles. Many books have been written on pastoral leadership, and new studies appear each year. Rather than attempt to address the vast literature on this subject, I will present briefly my position on the issue and wait for another time and place to elaborate more fully.

I believe the Scriptures teach kingdom principles that apply to the structure of the church in any social environment. The first of those principles is that independent power in the church belongs to Christ and to him alone. No church leader has independent power and authority to control knowledge, people, and resources. The second is that Christ delegated to the Twelve apostolic authority and power, from which they led the early church and, empowered by the Holy Spirit, gave to us the New Testament Scriptures. These same apostles delegated authority and power to subsequent generations of leaders, "full of the spirit and wisdom," to serve the needs of the local fellowship of believers. This delegated authority is always subject to the prior authority of Christ, of Scripture, and of a living senior generation of mature leaders whose lives have evidenced "the spirit and wisdom" of servant leadership.

At the same time, I see around the world pervasive evidence that the pattern of leadership and authority in the church always reflects the social context in which the church is planted. The plurality-of-elders model taught in some seminaries works well among the Aukan people, who have a social environment that allocates power and authority to elders in their community. The episcopal model, with the bishop and council or presbyters, works well in the social environment of the Yapese, where the hierarchist game defines key features of their traditional social organization. Yapese have little difficulty adapting the council of presbyters, holding both allocated and delegated power, since such councils are a common feature of their own social organization. The authoritarian pattern of leadership common in some Pentecostal groups, emphasizing independent and delegated power, has fit well with the authoritarian cultures of Latin America. Each of these patterns fails when people grasp social power, implicit in the relationships, rather than work in submission to the authority of Christ and the Scriptures.

In brief, a review of the history of the church with its many divisions and splits into denominations and subgroups illustrates the adaptability of the church to diverse variations in the social games of human societies. The argument here is that, beyond the kingdom principles outlined, there is no correct structure of authority taught in the Scriptures. No single organizational model is mandated or taught in Scripture. To the contrary, the organizational structure of the early church adapted to changing social contexts and needs.

Beyond the issue of structure, many texts in the New Testament address specifically the qualities, character, and expectations of church leaders. In Matthew 20 and Luke 22 Jesus discusses the issue of leadership with his disciples, noting that great men exercise authority over others, calling themselves benefactors. Jesus declares (Luke 22:25–27) that "you are not to be like that. Instead, the greatest among you should be like the youngest, and the one who rules like the one who serves. . . . I am among you as one who serves." In the cases presented the missionaries all too often appear as benefactors rather than as those who serve. This penchant grows not from an inherent carnality but rather is derived from the structure and values of their bureaucratic social roots and the position of economic power that they so often have in relation to their national co-workers.

We all use cultural metaphors of leadership. We typically draw these metaphors from some current cultural agenda for leadership. Christian colleges and universities employ the same metaphors of leadership—president, provost, dean, CEO, CAO— that occur in the wider academic culture. Mission organizations often draw upon the latest metaphors from business (MBO, entrepreneurial, cutting-edge, team-based). Churches have their special vocabulary (bishops, pastors, presbytery, synod), but the content of these concepts resembles that of president, senate, mayor, and council in the wider economic and political life of the culture. As Christians we need to rethink our roles through the metaphors of ministry employed in Scripture. Jesus typically calls his disciples servants, and Paul frequently refers to himself as a "servant of the Lord Jesus Christ." I wonder how Christian ministries might be transformed if their leaders began to speak of themselves in their daily discourse as followers, servants, witnesses, disciples, and shepherds of the flock of God.

Obviously, Christian leaders must exercise authority in the church. As we have illustrated, there are many different forms in which this authority may be exercised. The critical issue regarding authority in the church is not the form that authority takes but rather the manner and the motivation by which the leader exercises that responsibility. We lead through lives of pilgrimage, and the metaphors of Scripture provide our directional compass. As Bennett (1993) notes, the disciple is under authority rather than having authority over. Paul proclaims his authority as one for building up the brethren, not tearing them down or lording it over them. Paul calls Christians to be transformed by the renewing of their minds. Jesus calls disciples to identify with him, in his pattern of life and in his suffering. He does not impose a particular social system upon the church but rather calls his disciples to follow him, the good shepherd who cares for the sheep.

8

Disputes, Conflicts, and Communication

To Command or to Serve?

Case Studies

A Water Tank in Yap

During my field work on Yap I became involved in a dispute with the Yap Trading Company about money and labor on my water tank. In the initial plan to build a house, I contracted with the Yap Trading Company to hire a group of men to construct the house. That job proceeded well, and both the laborers and I were satisfied with the arrangement. They completed the house within the time schedule that we had agreed upon, and the money I paid was precisely stipulated in the contract.

Shortly after we moved into the house we decided to construct a water tank to provide a reliable supply of fresh water. The Filipino who was the head contractor for the Yap Trading Company agreed to construct a water tank for me. This time the men were paid by the hour rather than through a labor contract.

The two men assigned to build the water tank were clearly in no hurry to complete the job. From my perspective they took much too much time to bring the materials. When they actually began to work, they worked two or three hours during an eight-hour day. Of course, when the bill came for their labor I was charged for a full eight hours. I discovered, much to my chagrin, that it cost me more to have a water tank constructed than to build the whole house!

Being a graduate student at the time and working on a very limited income, I was furious. I went to the foreman at the Yap Trading Company and complained bitterly about the performance of these two men on this job. When I refused to pay the bill, the foreman told me I would have to talk to his boss.

The manager of the Yap Trading Company was a Yapese man who had earned his degree in business and who had returned to Yap to assume this management position. He was approximately ten years older than I, from a middle-level village in the Yap social structure.

I was angry and self-righteous. I believed that the laborers intended to cheat me and that the men in management were happy to let them do this so long as they were paid. Entering the manager's office with an aggressive, confrontive attitude, I approached his desk and after his courteous "What can I do for you?" I opened a verbal barrage of indignation and anger at the work of these two men and the audacity of the Yap Trading Company to bill me for labor that they had not done.

The manager sat quietly and listened to my tirade. When I was finished he reviewed silently some figures on his desk and then offered me a price for their labor that was half of what they had originally charged. When he asked if that would be agreeable to me, I was delighted. I had not anticipated such a reduction and was ecstatic to see this problem resolved so readily. I quickly wrote a check for the balance due, and we agreed that the bill was paid in full. I left the office victoriously.

Nearly a year later, after I had mastered the Yapese language to the point where I could work without interpreters, I attended the annual sessions of the Yap district legislature. The manager of the Yap Trading Company was a member of the legislature and participated in the meetings that I was actively observing. At the end of these legislative sessions the legislature had a party, and I was invited to be their guest. During this party I had the occasion to sit next to the manager.

Since parties of this kind generally involve the consumption of rather large quantities of beer, the manager had drunk enough to allow him to lose his ordinary caution and restraint. As I sat next to him he turned to me and began asking me questions. "Why do you Americans come here to study us?" He then suggested that I was arrogant, demanding my way and expecting that the Yapese should bow and scrape, doing what I pleased. He made it clear that I was not the kind of person that he wanted to have visiting on Yap, and he would be very happy if I would leave. They had helped me in the legislature not because I deserved it nor because I was a good person but rather because of my American status and my association with that power structure in their midst. He concluded that I was a typical American who came uninvited, pushed the Yapese around, insisted that things be done my way, and had no sincere interest or concern for the people themselves.

At that moment I realized that the confrontation nearly a year before had produced an enemy who retained significant animosity and hostility toward me. By this time, having learned more about Yapese society and social relationships, I recognized that I had indeed been pushy and aggressive and merited all of the negative assessment given to me. When I tried to apologize, it was of no avail. My character was evident, and excuses could never make up for my behavior on that occasion.

Only years later have I fully understood the significance of my actions and the inappropriateness of my behavior. The manner in which Yapese settle disputes and the manner in which they conduct themselves in conflict with one another are extremely different from that of my own social game. My behavior on that occasion, no matter how justified in my own eyes, was totally inappropriate and unacceptable to the Yapese. The manager's judgment of my character was consistent within the context of his own culture.

Disputes among the Deni Indians

Upon arriving in a Deni village in the Purus River region of the upper Amazon in Brazil, I took up residence in a thatch-roofed house in the center of the village. The second night I was awakened at about four o'clock in the morning by loud shouting that seemed to be inside my house. I sat upright and, as I became oriented to my surroundings, recognized that the voice was coming from the neighbor's house just behind me. He continued to speak in a loud, argumentative voice for the next ten minutes. When he finally stopped talking another man responded from a house across the village plaza. His voice was much quieter, but I detected an intensity in his response as well. Over the next hour I listened to people speaking back and forth from their hammocks in the early morning darkness.

At daybreak I left my house and walked across the plaza to the Koops' house. I asked Gordon what all the commotion was about that early in the morning. To my dismay, he had slept through the whole thing and told me that he had long ago learned to ignore these early-morning discussions. My curiosity would not rest, however, and I asked him to discover the explanation for this rather vehement early-morning conversation.

Later in the day Gordon told me that the man speaking by my house was one of the two village chiefs. He was complaining about women in the village who continued to pester him for a black, sticky substance used to glue feathers in their traditional headdresses and to manufacture other craft items. Frustrated that these women sat in the village while he worked in the forest, he resented their frequent requests to him and his wife for something they could collect themselves. He angrily refused to give any more glue to those who asked him. The other man in the village echoed his complaint and criticized those who had taken his things without asking.

After several days in the village I discovered that this early-morning public confrontation was not at all unusual. One afternoon I observed a man sitting on the top step of his house, shouting vehemently at another man across the village plaza. Soon the object of his scorn responded to him, and both of them carried on a loud public debate over the next hour. The first man accused the other of having an affair with his wife. The other man denied the accusation, and they battled verbally until both were exhausted from the dispute. During their argument others in the village from time to time gathered next to them and participated in the shouting match. The argument continued until all parties tired and disappeared into their houses.

Disputes, Conflict, and Social Games

Confrontation and Confrontation Avoidance

The two case studies illustrate two distinct methods of handling social conflict. In the Yapese situation my open confrontation not only offended my Yapese host but also destroyed any possible relationship with that individual. My style of handling a dispute and managing interpersonal conflict was so offensive that I have not to this day been able to rebuild that relationship. In stark contrast, the Deni Indians in Brazil not only engage in open confrontation and conflict but also expect outsiders to express their frustrations and their grievances publicly. How can we explain such drastic differences in procedures for settling disputes? What is the nature of the social games that characterize each of these societies, and what can we learn by a comparative study of such social environments?

The first obvious distinction in the two case studies is the difference in the management of confrontation. Open confrontation is unacceptable in Yap society. The manager of the Yap Trading Company not only resented my open confrontation but also was unable to respond until he was under the influence of alcohol. This is a common pattern in Yapese society; people avoid confrontation as much as possible until or unless they are drunk. To confront others when one is sober is inexcusable. People recognize that drunks cannot control themselves and therefore excuse them when they do what is otherwise socially unacceptable.

The Deni, in contrast, handle conflicts by open confrontation. When individuals find fault with others in the village they demonstrate their displeasure publicly in face-to-face conflict. This conflict is not without rules; to the contrary, many social conventions govern this confrontation.

These differences in approach to confrontation reflect differences in emphasis on the importance of the group as opposed to individuals. Yapese value the dignity of other persons and seek to maintain good relationships within the group. The Deni are strongly individualistic and openly promote individual interests and rights.

Each of these societies takes a significantly different approach to individual vulnerability. Yapese people see vulnerability as a weakness (Lingenfelter and Mayers 1986, 106); they exercise extreme care to protect the vulnerability of individuals and to avoid behaviors that provoke interpersonal conflict within the group. This is not to say they do not engage in conflict; the Yapese have a long history of extragroup conflict. However, relationships within the group are carefully regulated, and unity and solidarity of the group have extremely high value for Yapese.

The Deni, in contrast, are openly critical and are willing to expose vulnerability (Lingenfelter and Mayers 1986, 107–8). They denounce individual failures publicly and criticize one another in open debate over issues of importance to them.

The second key difference between the Yapese and Deni is the distinction between working through channels and engaging in face-to-face resolution of conflict. The Yapese define relationships hierarchically and manage disputes through the hierarchy. The Filipino foreman could not make a decision about the bill for my water tank. Instead, he asked that I go to his manager. My later understanding of the situation suggests that I should have sent a mediator to conduct my case with the manager. Such a person could facilitate a decision on my behalf without the intense alienation produced by my own open confrontation. Yapese pursue appropriate channels to achieve a favorable decision, applying pressure from the hierarchy to prod someone who may be obstructing or to enlist support of someone who has the power to make a decision on another's behalf. Going through channels is the appropriate means of managing conflict in Yapese culture and society. A mediator works through those channels to bring about a favorable decision.

The Deni, in contrast, engage in face-to-face confrontation and negotiation. The concept of channels is completely alien in their social environment. Deni operate in a web of personal relationships and influence. Motivated primarily by their personal interests and guided by shared values of what constitutes public good, individuals negotiate their own disputes and draw upon the support of family, friends, and neighbors. When one's web of influence is weak, the individual may choose to flee from a conflict rather than risk prolonged harassment by a stronger opponent.

These communication procedures and emphases reflect once again the influence of hierarchy and group in the social environment. The Deni value individual autonomy rather than group solidarity. The Yapese place every person in an elaborate hierarchy and assert the importance of group conformity. These contrasting values are reflected in the procedures that are acceptable to these societies for communicating in situations of conflict and dispute.

The Chain and the Net

The authoritarian and hierarchist social games, which emphasize hierarchy, have certain features in common and yet also significant differences.

The social organization of the universities in which I have worked is a bureaucratic version of the authoritarian game (fig. 8.1). The organization of the hierarchy is conceptualized as a chain of command. Most organizations of this type have as a significant part of their organizational structure a hierarchical chart showing the offices that are at the top of the command structure and all of those reporting to them in a continuously expanding chain of subordinate relationships. The chain is pyramidal in structure; a central office at the top has power over all of the offices beneath. Authority in this type of social setting is vertical. Information is passed through certain channels. If someone should have the audacity to go around the link that is above, people occupying the intermediate levels will become angry and frustrated with both the individual avoiding their authority and the higher officials who have allowed that person to engage in such practice. The integrity of the chain is based upon each link fulfilling its obligation to be subordinate to the link above and superordinate over the links below. Individuals who consistently refuse to go through channels may be subjected to severe social criticism and punitive action by other members of the system.

Individuals who have grievances confront their adversaries through appropriate channels, usually seeking a win/lose decision. Each individual attempts to gain a favorable decision and feels that he or she has lost if the decision is made against him or her. People who feel they have been treated unjustly may appeal their decisions and seek further arbitration at a higher level.

Figure 8.1

Social Games and Disputes

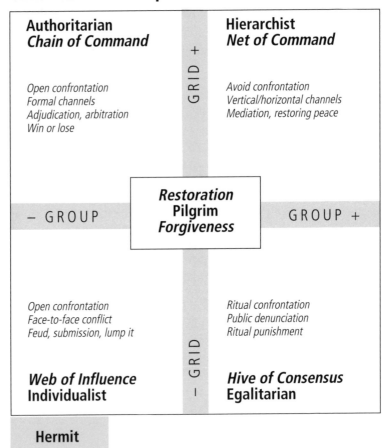

While Yapese society shares this preoccupation with hierarchy and channels, the importance of group in its social game creates a significantly different version of communication and decision-making processes (see fig. 8.1). The Yapese hierarchi-

cal structure is more like a net than a chain. The Yapese describe
the links between their different communities and leaders as
tha, or strings. These strings link villages and titled estates in
both vertical and horizontal planes. Information in the Yap system can travel both vertically and horizontally. The Yapese not
only find it appropriate to go around someone who is blocking
them but also have means of circumventing individuals and
offices that are obstructing them. Going through channels on
Yap means utilizing both vertical and horizontal relationships
to accomplish objectives, and mediators play a key role in facil-
itating this process.

The Web of Influence

The Deni reflect an individualist social game in which hierarchy and regulated communication of information to others
are insignificant. Deni operate upon a web of relationships and
face-to-face negotiations. The best that a Deni Indian chief can
do is to acquire authority through personal influence. Individuals who engage in regular economic and social exchanges often
support one another during situations of conflict.

In spite of thoroughgoing individualism the Deni hold common beliefs about the public good. These ideals define appropriate behavior for people within the community, and people
use them as standards of measurement against which the behavior of others in the community is judged. The Deni value "good
talk" and sharing that which they have gained through hunting
or farming in the community. When individuals violate these
standards of public good people exert social pressure upon them
to conform.

The resolution of conflict is always face-to-face negotiation.
Individuals fight to the point of exhaustion or until they agree
to establish "good talk" once again with one another. If the conflict cannot be resolved the weaker party may withdraw to a
safer place some distance from the village. We observed that
people who withdrew from the village returned after several
days, when they were certain that the intensity of the conflict
had died down. To accomplish reconciliation, they first com-

municated their desire to reestablish "good talk" and then resumed ordinary social and economic activities.

The Hive of Consensus

The Aukan are unlike the Yapese in that they do not have significant hierarchical relationships and unlike the Deni in that they place strong emphasis on the group at the expense of the individual. Their egalitarian social environment is analogous to a beehive, in which everyone has similar work, individuals are not distinguished from one another, and the collective has far greater value than the individual. The ancestors constitute the ever-present queen of the hive.

Aukan elders, men and women, hold the knowledge and traditions of the community and act as defenders of the communal good. No one individual has the power to command or direct. However, those individuals who are the captains and the elders articulate the consensus decisions of the group.

The Aukan have clear standards as to what is desirable and appropriate for the good of the community. These ideas of public good are much more carefully defined than are those in Deni society, and the boundaries and interests of the group are more clearly articulated. Those who choose to violate group norms may be excluded permanently from the group. Individuals gain support for their personal interests by demonstrating their commitment to the public good and to the interest of the group as a whole. Decision making is based upon group consensus, and individuals are expected to conform to these group decisions.

The Aukan, like the Yapese, avoid conflict as much as possible. Confrontation occurs through the mediation of diviners. An individual Aukaner will not directly confront another Aukaner in a public dispute. Instead, people allow social insults and injuries to lie below the surface of relations until they experience bad luck or illness. At that point the person who has experienced a disaster or an illness will seek the counsel of a diviner to find out what or who is the cause of that particular problem. The diviner is the broker for the settlement of conflict and dispute in Aukan society. The diviner determines through ritual what wrongs the person has done and which of the spirits or ancestors or the living are punishing this individual for wrong-doing. Illness, disaster, and other misfortunes are all punitive actions from the perspective of the Aukaner.

Ritual confrontation in egalitarian societies takes many different forms. Public gossip is the simplest, and an early warning form of confrontation. Like the buzzing of angry bees, gossip warns offenders that they are a danger to the group. When this is not effective people move to higher-risk forms of indirect confrontation. Among animists sorcery or the threat of sorcery is common, whereas people in literate societies confront or threaten through anonymous letters, newsletters, or e-mail and electronic bulletin boards. The Amish have at times chosen to confront by shunning a person, or refusing to speak in any circumstance. If these techniques do not accomplish the persons' or group's objective of discipline or correction, and the offense is great enough to warrant group action, the ultimate action is a public "stinging" in which the group confronts the person openly, with extreme consequences such as banishing the person from the group.

Managing Conflict in Ministry

To Confront or Not to Confront: The Missionary in Deni Society

Early in their ministry with the Deni, the Koops found that the Indians were extremely curious about the sexuality of their children. When the children went out of the house to the nearby toilet, Deni men and women often followed them and touched their private parts. This created a great deal of concern and tension for the parents. Anxious about their children's safety, they decided that the children must not go out alone. From that time on they confined the children to the house during the months of village living and allowed them to go out into the public places only when they were accompanied by a parent.

This limited interaction between the Koops and the community was deeply distressing to the Koops. They found it hard to keep their children confined to the house for long periods of time, and yet they were anxious about them being in the village.

Concerned that their Christian testimony would be lost if they confronted the Deni, they resigned themselves to isolation, knowing no other way to resolve the problem.

The solution to the Koops' problem lay at their doorstep, but because of their own cultural values they were unable to utilize it. When I asked Gordon Koop why he did not confront the Deni openly and shout at them from his porch step about these matters he could not imagine that such behavior would be accepted, nor was it in any way appropriate from his point of view. From his own culture of origin in Canada displays of public anger are un-Christian.

Seeing that the Koops were not able to bring themselves to shout at their neighbors, I began to look for an opportunity where I could illustrate the power and effectiveness of using this strategy for settling disputes. One afternoon we had been working on the airstrip. Nearly exhausted from the heat, I decided to go to a nearby stream and bathe. When I reached the bathing area nearest to our house I discovered that several women and children were already bathing and playing in the water. Since Deni women bathed in the nude, Gordon and I did not feel comfortable entering a stream where they were bathing. I turned around and crossed over the airstrip to find a more distant stream where I could soak in peace. As I neared the second bathing area I heard the voices of women and children coming from the water. In my frustration I decided that this was an opportune time to test my hypothesis about conflict resolution. I began to shout at the top of my voice in English, which of course the Deni did not understand. I complained that the women were lazy, that they spent hours in the afternoon bathing while the men were hard at work on the airstrip. Feeling gratified with at least the opportunity to shout in my frustration, I began a lengthy exhortation in English. Within two or three minutes, a Deni woman and her children hurried toward me on the path. In quick succession several others followed. Within minutes I had the stream all to myself and sank with great pleasure into the cool, refreshing water.

That evening one of the women came to visit us. With great delight and humor she recounted to Gordon the afternoon's incident. As she told him how I scolded and scolded, she related how everyone laughed afterward and how at last they had begun to understand this foreigner. As Gordon related the story to me, it was clear to both of us that my shouting had not in any way damaged our standing in the community but rather had enhanced it.

Indirect Decision Making: The Power of Contextualized Behavior in Yap

Mediation is a key process by which Yapese settle disputes. However, similar principles operate for routine decision making in Yapese society. A few years ago I received a letter from one of my missionary friends on Yap who asked how he could be more effective in drawing Yapese men into leadership and decision-making roles in the local evangelical church.

I related to him an incident that I had experienced in the late 1960s. I had not yet learned the Yapese language and was dependent upon my language teacher to translate for me. We were sitting in his home village in the local men's house where the men engaged in extended discussion.

One of the elder men initiated the subject by saying, "I have an idea, but it will take a lot of tin." Another man in the meeting responded by saying, "It takes a lot of money to get tin. Only a few of us are working in town. Can you young guys help us buy tin?" The discussion then progressed around the subject of money, wage work, and buying tin. After more than a half-hour of dialogue on this subject, they concluded that they could not afford a lot of tin, and that ended the discussion.

I asked my Yapese interpreter to explain the meaning of the conversation. He said, "Oh, it's very simple. The first man wanted to build a community house, but he couldn't say it. If he had stated that he had an idea of building a community house, no one in the meeting could have disagreed with him." He explained that everyone knew that the village needed a community house; it was humiliating to be without such a building. If he had stated this openly, the others could not disagree with him. The word would have immediately spread that the leaders in the village had decided to build a community house. In fact they were not ready to make such a decision, and if they had said no they would have been humiliated publicly. They would be further humiliated if they had said yes and did not build it.

I then suggested to the enquiring missionary that the standard operating procedure of Western missionaries is to present their agenda in public to church leaders. In the Yap evangelical church these leaders come from the same cultural background as those men in the men's house. They are extremely reluctant to disagree with a missionary and feel embarrassed to reject what they know are worthy ideas for the church. As a consequence, they readily agree with the missionary's agenda but often fail to support its implementation.

An alternative approach to decision making is to follow their example. Suppose the Yapese church needed new paint. The missionary might suggest that the church is looking shabby in comparison to the other churches in town. He can make this comment to several of the elders on a one-to-one basis rather than in a public meeting. As he makes his comment and listens to their feedback the idea is sown as a seed for them to think about and to discuss independently. If they themselves begin to see that this is a problem and decide they want to do something about it they will raise the issue at some future meeting. At that point, however, the decision will already have been made. When the elders raise an issue in a meeting they have already discussed it with one another and are ready to move ahead and mobilize the people to accomplish what they have proposed.

The enquiring missionary accepted my suggestion and began to try to work with Yapese leaders using this indirect decision process. After just a few attempts to implement this strategy he was sharply criticized by another missionary colleague. The colleague told him that he was being devious and dishonest. The critic argued that talking to people individually was setting up a situation so that a decision would be made in his favor. The indirect strategy denied the Yapese a fair opportunity to disagree with him and to object to his point of view.

The disagreement between these two men reflects a basic misunderstanding of the issue. The critic accused the enquirer of predetermining the decision. In fact the strategy of the critic had precisely that effect: by bringing an issue to the attention of the Yapese congregation in a public setting, their own cultural rules forbade disagreement and therefore assured an affirmative decision. Private dialogue allows them to think, talk, and even disagree with the missionary on a one-to-one basis.

The key to this behavior in Yapese society is the importance of consensus decision making in the group. Individuals may disagree with one another on a one-to-one basis, but when they are in a setting where the group process is at work, the desire and need for consensus are so great that individuals who have dissenting views will be silent rather than risk the disfavor of the group.

Missionaries must be willing to risk their own values and concept of process. To follow Western ideas of process in Yapese society is to result in the breakdown of decision making and the loss of public support. To win the support of these people it is necessary to rely on the indirect decision model that they use for their own public process.

Pilgrim Principles for Situations of Social Risk

Many missionaries with whom I have worked in Third-World contexts derive their structures for communication and processes for handling disputes from their personal, cultural background and through interpretations of Scripture derived from those roots. The typical pattern for conflict resolution is the authoritarian game interpretation of Matthew 18:15–17. The missionary interprets this text as a universal process without reference to the social environment in which the command was given or to the social environment in which it is to be applied. Usually the command "If your brother sins against you, go and show him his fault, just between the two of you" is interpreted as a command to confront, face to face and privately. No other passage of Scripture is relevant, no other references are considered, and the missionary attempts to put this into practice in any social game encountered. When the personal confrontation fails, they employ the strategy implied in the statement to "take one or two others along, so that every matter may be established by the testimony of two or three witnesses." If that fails, they bring the full authority of the church to bear on the matter in a public and confrontational way.

Many evangelicals fail to see that this text is written to a specific group of people in a specific social game applying universal kingdom principles for specific social action. Confusing procedure with principle and form with meaning, they attempt to resolve all situations of conflict with a culturally specific formula. But if we view Matthew 18:15–17 as a metaphor rather than a method consistent with the other metaphors in the same text, then we may ask, What key principles implied in this text may be extended to any social game? Is the form prescribed appropriate to the social environment in which the conflict occurs? How can a missionary or a national believer follow Jesus within the local social environment and culture?

The first kingdom principle is to exercise caution and wisdom in situations of conflict by restricting the scope of the disagreement to "just between the two of you." In the Old Testament wisdom literature, we find many proverbs instructing people to exercise caution. "Do not accuse a man for no reason" (Prov. 3:30); "It is to a man's honor to avoid strife" (Prov. 20:3); "What you have seen with your eyes do not bring hastily to court" (Prov. 25:8).

The second principle is to restore relationships with those with whom we have disagreement. In Matthew 22:39 Jesus affirms the centrality of the Old Testament command to "love your neighbor as yourself." This command is repeated numerous times in the epistles, and Paul reminds us to "do nothing out of selfish ambition or vain conceit, but in humility consider others better than yourselves" (Phil. 2:3).

The third principle is to humbly rely on the counsel of others rather than on personal judgment. The effect of bringing "two or three witnesses" is to invite their counsel as well as their support. James writes that we are to be quick to listen, slow to speak, and slow to anger (James 1:19). Paul admonishes us to "be completely humble and gentle; be patient, bearing with one another in love. Make every effort to keep the unity of the Spirit through the bond of peace" (Eph. 4:2–3). We are warned against quarreling about words (2 Tim. 2:14) and that jealousy and quarreling are products of worldliness (1 Cor. 3:3).

The fourth principle is forgiveness. In Matthew 18:21 Peter asks Jesus how often he should forgive a brother who sins against him. Peter suggests that "seven times" is enough. Jesus rejects Peter's offer as woefully inadequate, expanding it to "seventy times seven," and then tells a story about a certain king and his servant who asks for forgiveness. The servant receives forgiveness for a huge debt, only to turn and throw a fellow servant into prison for a minor debt. Because of the servant's failure to forgive when he had been forgiven for so much more, the king gave him over to torment until he paid all that was due. Jesus then connects the story to the forgiveness we have received from our heavenly Father and the judgment due to us should we not extend the same forgiveness to a brother who sins against us.

As I have illustrated in the opening case study in this chapter, face-to-face confrontation, even done privately, destroys unity and peace in Yapese society. Certainly I did not consider the Yapese manager better than myself, and I obviously failed to exercise caution and wisdom in that social environment. The outcome of my behavior was a relational disaster. As I have observed elsewhere (Lingenfelter and Mayers 1986, 112–16; Lingenfelter 1996, 256–61) mediation produces far more satisfactory outcomes in places like Yap.

As we explore New Testament passages, seeking guidance for the management of conflict within the church and between church and society, it is essential that we understand the social environment of the early church. The management of conflict in the Jewish and Greek worlds described in the Book of Acts is characterized by formal confrontation, majority rule, and arbitration or adjudication of disputes. These features grow out of a bureaucratic, authoritarian social game that typified the expanding, dispersing church.

The process described in Acts 15 is one in which there is formal, open confrontation on an issue. People publicly criticized one another and argued openly about the issue. Mediation was not part of the process. Confrontation continued until objections were silenced and no further argument was allowed. James had the authority to arbitrate the solution, which was not questioned. While the objections were silenced, the conflict did not end. Many dissidents carried on their crusade for circumcision and adherence to the law throughout the Gentile world.

Those who desire to be effective Christian leaders must understand the social games of the people to whom they minister and practice pilgrim leadership. The question of whether to confront, whether to use indirect or direct modes of decision making, or whether to use channels of authority or webs of relationship ought to be settled on the basis of social environment. Once the social game is understood, Christians must examine how they may live transformed lives, employing kingdom principles, renewing the quality of relationships, forgiving every offense, and engaging the people in that society to discover the unity of the Spirit and the bond of peace.

The Story: Christian Pilgrimage for Masaai Missionaries and Pastors

One day during a period of prolonged drought, a group of Masaai pastors and I (a Southern Baptist missionary) gathered in a local church to decide where we should go for evangelism. They, looking for a place with water and grass, said, "We want to go up to the Ngong Hills." Knowing that Presbyterian and Catholic churches have worked there for years, I said, "No! We've already been to that area. We should go to the Loodokilani area." One man, just as adamant, said, "No! We want to go to the Ngong Hills."

I am a professional at debate, so I jumped to the challenge: "No, we're not going there because . . ." and I started listing reasons, slapping my hand, pointing my finger, and calling the man's name. I vehemently rejected his ideas for going to this place.

As I carried on, the Masaai leaders, heads down, started to walk out of the church. I shouted, "Where are you guys going? This is important business. Why are you all leaving?"

Finally one brave soul said, "Because you're about to fight." Suddenly I realized something was wrong, and I said, "What do you mean we're about ready to fight?"

He said, "Look at your face and the way that you're shouting at him, and the way that you're whacking your hand. You're going to fight. And we're not going to be here when you fight, because when people fight they get hurt, and we're not going to get hurt."

You know I am a little slow. So I said, "Oh, wait a minute, I must be making a mistake. Have I sinned?" And they said, "Big time!"

Given as I am to extremes, I got down on my knees before them and said, "I'm sorry. I have sinned." They said, "Get up. Get off your knees." I said, "I didn't know I was doing anything wrong. I was just arguing like I did at home, like white people do. You look in their face, you make your point, and you make it with your hands. I'm sorry. Will you forgive me?" The man I had argued with said, "Okay."

Then I said, "I have to know something. How do you disagree? I have to learn how to disagree. I can't sit here and listen without knowing how to disagree."

So they began to explain to me. "Number one, you do NOT look a person in the eye. Number two, you do NOT call someone by name. Number three, you do NOT point your finger at the person you are disagreeing with. Number four, you do NOT raise your voice. Because when you raise your voice in Masaai land it's time for war, and in war people get hurt or killed. And, number five, do NOT address the subject directly."

I said, "Wait a minute. Let me see if I got this straight. I can't call their name, I can't look at them, I don't point my finger, I don't raise my voice, and I can't talk about the subject, so what can I do?"

"Well, if you were to tell a story about the situation and not mention any of the people in here or the situation, that would be best." I thought, "Oh, Lord have mercy!"

Not long after that (I thought I had it down, and by God's grace I would not argue again) we had a big disagreement about another evangelistic outreach. It was not between them and me; they were completely divided and arguing quietly among themselves.

I thought to myself, "Lord, I really need a story." I went out of the church and prayed. That church is near a mountain known for its many lions, and the Lord gave me a story as I prayed.

I went back into the church and said, "Did you men hear about the herders who went looking for the lions that killed their cows? Six guys were tracking some into the hills, and one of them got a thorn in his foot. His buddy [Masaai men usually have a buddy] asked the other four to stop so the injured man could get the thorn out of his foot. The other four said, 'No, we're not waiting on you. We're going on.'"

The pastors knew then that something was wrong . . . when you go hunt lions you hunt them together. You don't split up; you go as a group. I continued, "After the other four were out of sight, one lion circled back and killed the two men who had stopped."

At this point in the story the pastors were amazed and kept asking, "Who are these people?"

I continued, "The other four men went up into the mountain, where the tracks divided, some leading to a rocky place and others leading to the forest. They then had a big disagreement about which way they should go. One pair said, 'We should go this way to the rocks.' The others said, 'No, let's go this way to the forest.' So they split up again."

The pastors started shaking and lowering their heads; they knew this was not good as I concluded the story. "There were two lions, and they each turned and killed the two men tracking them."

The pastors yelled, "When did this happen?" I said, "It's happening right now, because the devil, the lion who goes about seeking whom he may devour, is doing that to us, causing us to be divided."

After some stunned silence, they said, "Ooooh. You're right." The argument ended, and we got down on our knees together and prayed, asking God for direction on which way to go. After prayer we agreed to send men into the Loodokilani area, which to our knowledge was largely unreached. Today we have five churches in that area, but had we remained divided, that would have never taken place.

And if I had not learned how to tell a story, we may have remained divided and at the mercy of the devouring lion.

9
Transforming Culture

The man who loves his life will lose it, while the man who hates his life in this world will keep it for eternal life. Whoever serves me must follow me; and where I am, my servant also will be. My Father will honor the one who serves me. (John 12:25–26)

Case Studies

Samuel, Saul, and Israel

The people of Israel pondered their dilemma. Samuel, their leader for more than four decades, seemed old, feeble, and unable to lead the people against their enemies as he had done in his youth. And, tragically, his sons lacked the character and godliness of their father. In the few years that they had served as appointed justices under Samuel they had accepted bribes and thus perverted justice. To make matters worse Nahash, an Ammonite king, proved a ruthless and powerful enemy. His army had raided and harassed Israelite towns near his border, and each year they threatened a wider area.

Finally the elders of Israel decided that the situation had reached crisis proportion, and they called a meeting at Ramah to discuss matters with Samuel. They were afraid! And they had good reason, threatened as they were by poor leadership, weak organization, and a big enemy. But they had a solution. They

proposed to Samuel that they adopt the hierarchist game of kingship, played among their enemies, and appoint a new leader to
lead them in their battles. They were confident that with better
organization and new leadership they could win this war against
Nahash.

After some grumbling and complaining, Samuel granted their
request. Within a few months he anointed Saul, a Benjamite and
a man of significant physical stature, as king over Israel. Soon
after his appointment as king Saul proved his worth. Nahash,
the Ammonite king, besieged the town of Jabesh Gilead, east of
the Jordan River. When Saul heard the report, the spirit of God
moved upon him in power, and he mobilized the armies of Israel
and defeated Nahash. With their primary enemy virtually
destroyed, the people of Israel celebrated their great fortune, their
wisdom in shifting from the egalitarian to the hierarchist game,
and King Saul as the new leader to replace Samuel (1 Sam. 8–11).

Midwest Bible Church

A few years ago the congregation of Midwest Bible Church
called a new pastor to lead it into the decade of the 1990s. The
congregation had recently renovated its facility in the center of
a small Midwestern city and had a thriving ministry with young
people and young adults. Approximately half of the congregation was made up of men and women who had been in the
church for twenty or more years, and many of these were senior citizens.

Pastor Absalom, having served for several years in a smaller
rural church following his graduation from seminary, accepted
the call to Midwest Bible Church. Within a few months of assum-
ing this ministry, he told the senior citizens in the church that
there was no place for them in his ministry plan. Using political means, he had several of the senior men removed from the
elder board and replaced them with people whom he felt were
loyal to his aspirations and ministry.

Looking at the urban setting of the church, Pastor Absalom
concluded that the location offered no future for ministry. The
neighborhood surrounding the church was filled with Cambo-
dian and other Asian immigrants and a growing population of

African-Americans. Pastor Absalom decided that the church must relocate to an area more suburban in character. The new and younger church board concurred with his decision, and they arranged with a realtor to list the church for sale. During that same time, the pastor and the board identified a particular location outside of the city where they planned a new worship facility.

Within a few years they sold the old property, built a new church in the suburbs, and relocated to this facility. However, the cost of the land and the new church building burdened the congregation with significant debt, and by the time the congregation had moved into the new facility the number attending had declined significantly. The pastor and the elders struggled over the next several years to rebuild the congregation in their new location. Yet attendance continued to decline, and finally the church failed to meet its mortgage payments or to pay the pastor's salary. At that point Pastor Absalom resigned, left the ministry, and abandoned the remnants of the congregation in their struggle to recover.

New Leadership, Better Organization

When people have significant problems in their work or ministry communities they, like the people of Israel, often seek a solution through restructuring their organization and changing leadership. Usually these changes have positive effect for a time on the community and lead to a resolution of some of the significant and aggravating problems. As long as the leader continues to be effective and the organization and community achieve their goals, people are content with the status quo. However, when the leader ages or the community goes through a period of unanticipated crisis, people again evaluate their leadership and their social game.

This pattern is repeated in the history of church and mission organizations. Hudson Taylor served for a time in China under a well-established British missionary agency. Frustrated with its policies and aggravated because he did not have the freedom to pursue a ministry in the manner that he deemed appropriate, he returned to England and established his own church base and mission organization, the China Inland Mission. With new leadership and a change in organizational structure, the China Inland Mission became a powerful force for evangelism in the early twentieth century.

Following World War II, young veterans returning home had a new passion and vision for world evangelism. However, they deemed the existing mission organizations inadequate and unresponsive to the great opportunities and great needs in the postwar period. Dick Hillis, William Cameron Townsend, Bob Bowman and many others started new organizations with specific missions and a particular social game that each of these men felt would be most suitable to the evangelistic ministry he envisioned. All of them were in large part successful and had a major impact for world evangelism. However, forty or fifty years later these founding leaders are gone, and young people entering into the mission force often judge these old organizations as unresponsive and inadequate for the needs of the 1990s.

The Fallacy of a Better Game

In every generation people decide that the old leaders and the old game are inadequate. What they need are new leaders and a new social game to make ministry happen.

Samuel's harvest sermon to the people of Israel, after the great victory that Saul had enjoyed over Nahash, the Ammonite king, provides a powerful critique of this mentality. In this sermon, Samuel acknowledges that they have a new leader and a better organization, the kingship. And then he reminds them of their short memory. It was the Lord who called Moses and Aaron, and they delivered the people out the hands of Pharaoh. It was the Lord who sent Jerub-Baal (NIV), Barak, Jephthah, and Samuel to deliver the people in their recent history. All of this they had forgotten when their fear of Nahash overpowered them. Samuel reminded the people that the only one that they should fear is the Lord. "If you fear the LORD and serve and obey him and do not rebel against his commands, and if both you and the king who reigns over you follow the LORD your God—good! But if you do not obey the LORD, and if you rebel against his commands, his hand will be against you, as it was against your fathers" (1 Sam. 12:14–15).

The conclusion of Samuel's story is that success is not contingent upon leadership and social game. Fear of the Lord and faithful service are God's primary requirements. "But be sure to fear the LORD and serve him faithfully with all your heart; consider what great things he has done for you. Yet if you persist in doing evil, both you and your king will be swept away" (1 Sam. 12:24–25). When we make our social games and our leadership our idols, they become useless.

The Danger of Idolatry

"Do not be afraid," Samuel replied. "You have done all this evil; yet do not turn away from the LORD, but serve the LORD with all your heart. Do not turn away after useless idols. They can do you no good, nor can they rescue you, because they are useless. For the sake of his great name the LORD will not reject his people, because the LORD was pleased to make you his own. As for me, far be it from me that I should sin against the LORD by failing to pray for you. And I will teach you the way that is good and right." (1 Sam. 12:20–23)

The people of Israel turned away from God to trust a political regime of kingship and a new leader to deliver them from their problems. Samuel reminded them that neither a king nor his army could deliver them from their enemies. And Samuel warned them against the idolatry that comes when people turn away from God and seek their solutions in other things. Tragically, idolatry of this kind is common in mission and church ministries.

The demise of Pastor Absalom and Midwest Bible Church is the result of idolatry. Like the people of Israel, this congregation believed that a new leader, a better organization, a new building, and a new location would bring about the blessing of God and create a mighty, expanding church. However, Pastor Absalom trusted more in his own wisdom than in the power of God. He refused to listen to counsel from his elders, he insisted upon a plan he was certain would provide success, and he led his people into debt, decline, and the destruction of what had been a dynamic ministry in the community where the church had historically served.

The greater tragedy is that this congregation sat debt-free in the midst of a great mission field in this small Midwestern city. In the community surrounding the congregation there were literally thousands of people who did not know the name of the Lord Jesus Christ and who were open for evangelistic outreach and ministry. Rather than reach out to these people, Pastor Absalom fled the scene, seeking to perpetuate a middle-class church in a middle-class suburb with middle-class models of ministry. The history of Midwest Bible Church is like the history of Israel, where the people and their king were swept away.

The Way of the Cross

Throughout this book we have seen examples of mission organizations and churches each embracing a particular social game. While the members of these organizations are for the most part believers and have committed themselves to being disciples and followers of the Lord Jesus Christ, their ministry and practice typically reflect the values of the social game of the culture of which they are a part. Cross-cultural workers carry their social values and expectations with them. When they establish new ministries they often find the role of the learner too slow and too difficult for their taste and insist upon transplanting the organization and values that they have carried from their home communities. The more tightly they hold on to these social values, the more prone they are to idolatry, depending upon their systems rather than fearing the Lord.

Most Christian workers have so overlearned their cultural values that they confuse them with the teaching of Scripture. They are blind to the passages of Scripture that contradict their point of view, and they are skilled in rationalizing their values through proof-texts from their Bible study. They read the indictments of the Pharisees in the New Testament as blind guides but would be loath to apply the same indictments to themselves and their ministries.

Jesus sharply rebuked the Pharisees and his own disciples. The only avenue of freedom from the bondage of culture is the cross. "If anyone would come after me, he must deny himself and take up his cross daily and follow me. For whoever wants to save his life will lose it, but whoever loses his life for me will save it. What good is it for a man to gain the whole world, and yet lose or forfeit his very self?" (Luke 9:23–25). All of the social games fade in their significance in the light of the cross, and all become subject to a higher priority, transformed submission to Jesus in a life of pilgrimage (see fig. 9.1).

The cross of Jesus Christ overshadows culture, shaping the life of the church. The message of the cross is sacrifice, suffering, and death to the things of the world. Jesus talks about hating one's life and losing it for the kingdom of God. As Samuel deplored the kingship in Israel as a source of salvation for the people, so Jesus deplored the egalitarian games of the Zealots and the Pharisees and the hierarchist games of the Sadducees and the Romans. He warned his disciples that the only way that they could follow him was to hate the social games of their family, community, and national life (Luke 14:26–33).

The Church: God's Agency for Transformation

From the day of Pentecost, when the Holy Spirit moved with power upon the small band of disciples in Jerusalem, the church has been God's agency for the transformation of cultures and societies. From the beginning the vitality of the church has rested in the empowering of the Holy Spirit and the obedience of its members for the proclamation of the gospel and the discipling of new believers. We read in the Book of Acts that the new believers devoted themselves daily to the teaching of the disciples, fellowship, the breaking of bread, and prayer (Acts 2:42). These spiritual disciplines were part of the shaping of the people of God.

As the church spread out of Jerusalem in response to persecution, its power was based upon the collective spiritual life of its members and their commitment to being followers of the Lord Jesus Christ. They endured persecution and hardship and boldly preached the gospel to anyone who would listen. Moving

Figure 9.1
The Way of the Cross

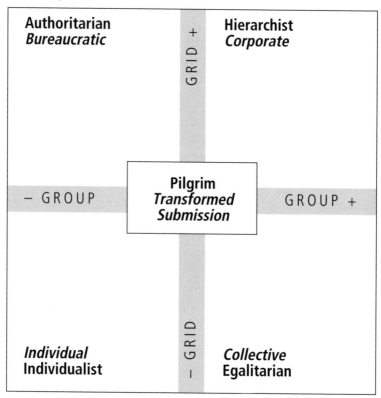

outward, proclaiming good news in the power of the Holy Spirit, they touched every people group with the message of hope, love, and reconciliation to God. As they followed the commands of the Lord Jesus before his death, their love and fearlessness in the face of opposition impressed the weak and the powerful in the pagan world around them. "A new command I give you: Love one another. As I have loved you, so you must love one another. All men will know that you are my disciples, if you love one another" (John 13:34–35).

Empowered by the Holy Spirit and living lives in the spirit that produced love, joy, peace, long-suffering, gentleness, goodness, and faith, they began to change the world of the Jews and the Greeks around them. There was much opposition and conflict in this change process. Unbelievers resisted them fiercely, defending the old cultures, attempting to stamp out the evangelists and their converts whose lives refuted the integrity and vitality of the existing cultural systems.

Pilgrim Churches

Cultural transformation has never come easily. The first church in Jerusalem was torn by the division between those who insisted upon the perpetuation of a Jewish culture and world and those like Peter, Paul, and Barnabas, who in the power of the Spirit began to recognize that their tradition was an empty way of life handed to them by their ancestors. It was Peter who ultimately framed this tension in his epistle to believers, "God's elect," strangers scattered abroad in the Greek world. Peter is the one who reminded them that they were purchased by the precious blood of Christ and given freedom from the "empty way of life" of their ancestors.

In the power of the Holy Spirit, Peter proclaimed these new believers "living stones" and "a spiritual house." These two metaphors capture the essence of what it means to be a pilgrim church. The pilgrim church is made of flesh and blood, not of fine cut stone, great arches, or stained-glass windows. The church is a spiritual house, not a great cathedral or a place where the great of this world are buried in splendor. The people who make up this great edifice in their natural state have no claim at all to being a people. They come from many different ethnic groups, from many different localities; they play every social game and speak thousands of languages. Peter says clearly that they were not a people, but now they have become a people of God (1 Peter 2).

The great metaphor that runs throughout the epistle of Peter is that of the crucified Jesus Christ. We are consecrated by the sprinkled blood of Christ. Our freedom was bought by the precious blood of Christ. Jesus is the stone rejected by men but choice and precious in the sight of God. Jesus suffered on our behalf and through that suffering left us an example that we should follow. Abused, he did not respond with abuse. Suffering, he did not threaten, but in all these things he committed his cause to "him who judges justly." "He himself bore our sins in his body on the tree . . . by his wounds you have been healed" (1 Peter 2:21–24). Peter concludes, "Since Christ suffered in his body, arm yourselves also with the same attitude, because he who has suffered in his body is done with sin" (1 Peter 4:1).

Pilgrim living becomes possible when we have indeed finished with sin and armed ourselves with the mind of Christ to endure suffering. We are then able to live not for our desires but for what God wills. We are empowered to lead an ordered, sober life, given to prayer. We are able to love one another, and to be hospitable, using our gifts in service.

The metaphor that Peter gives us for leadership is taken directly from the life and ministry of Jesus Christ. Peter calls Jesus the shepherd and guardian of our souls, and he challenges us "as a fellow elder, a witness of Christ's sufferings and one who also will share in the glory to be revealed: Be shepherds of God's flock that is under your care, serving as overseers—not because you must, but because you are willing, as God wants you to be; not greedy for money, but eager to serve; not lording it over those entrusted to you, but being examples to the flock. And when the Chief Shepherd appears, you will receive the crown of glory that will never fade away" (1 Peter 5:1–4).

The essence of pilgrim living and pilgrim leadership is submission to one another in Christ. Peter calls for believers to submit themselves to every authority instituted, for wives to submit themselves to their husbands, and for young men to submit to those who are older. Peter concludes, "Clothe yourselves with humility toward one another, because, 'God opposes the proud but gives grace to the humble'" (1 Peter 5:5).

The Cost of Sin

In the late 1970s the pastoral leaders in a West African denomination of churches formed a partnership with a Bible translation mission organization to translate the Bible into their language. One particular community of this language group provided the leadership for the translation project, and several key pastors provided the motivation and leadership for this enterprise. Early in the translation process, the pastors formed a committee to oversee the raising of funds and the organization of the program within their church community.

When the pastors brought the translation project before their churches, people embraced the idea of having the Bible in their language. Pastors took up offerings in their local churches and gathered a modest sum of money to provide local support. However, within a few short months these leaders withdrew their support, and the churches ceased giving to the program.

The Bible translation organization sent in a research team to talk to church leaders and committee members to discern why. After extensive interviews among people in the community, the research team reported widespread dissatisfaction with how the committee managed their funds. In this particular region of West Africa people saved their money in voluntary savings societies. People had rigorous standards for managing savings, and the savings societies had a fine record of accountability and performance. The research team discovered that the Bible translation committee had placed all of its funds in the hands of one man, Pastor Samson, the secretary-treasurer, who also utilized those funds to pay himself for Bible translation work. While the position of secretary-treasurer was common in church committees, the local culture prescribed significantly different rules for the management of funds in the savings societies.

The research team heard accusations that Pastor Samson used committee funds for fuel for his motorbike and for personal needs. The mission team in the community also complained that Pastor Samson took his wages but did not complete translation work in accord with their mutual agreement.

The research team recommended that the Bible translation committee adopt the standards and practices of the local savings societies in its management of funds. However, Pastor Samson, the secretary-treasurer who had personal access to the funds without accountability, resisted this change. The mission team decided to change its practices, however, and instead of giving funds directly to the committee began paying for translation work completed rather than an hourly wage.

Twenty years later the team completed the translation of the New Testament. Pastor Samson, who had been accused of the misuse of funds early in the project, had continued to serve effectively as one of the key translators in the program. Now chairman of the translation committee, he continued to exercise control over the resources and finances of the committee. Shortly after the translation was dedicated and distribution of the Scriptures commenced, Pastor Samson was accused of adultery. He denied those accusations but subsequently was disciplined by his colleagues and removed from the leadership of the translation committee and the church. However, Pastor Samson had carefully kept in his own possession all of the copies of the translated Scripture and other materials published for distribution by the committee. He refused to allow distribution of any of the published materials apart from his control.

The tragedy of this story is that the translation of God's Word into this language will always be tainted by the character issues surrounding Pastor Samson. Early in his ministry the people questioned his integrity with regard to money. The pattern of greed and self-service was never resolved and continued to undermine his effectiveness in ministry. In spite of this flaw, he was very well educated and clearly gifted for the work of Bible translation. Yet the conclusion of his translation service was marred even more than its beginning, with the accusation of and the discipline for adultery. Pastor Samson used his leadership role to lord it over the translation committee and over those who sought to hold him accountable for the sake of the integrity of the church and the gospel.

Sin is incredibly damaging to any Christian community. Peter warns us, "Be self-controlled and alert. Your enemy the devil prowls around like a roaring lion looking for someone to devour. Resist him, standing firm in the faith, because you know that your brothers throughout the world are undergoing the same kind of sufferings" (1 Peter 5:8–9).

Throughout this book we have been focusing on issues of cultural conflict and misunderstanding. Oftentimes people use the cloak of cultural misunderstanding to cover selfishness and sin. Sin in the life of the missionary, the pastor, or any Christian worker undermines and destroys the ministry and the community of the people of God.

Peter reminds us that we must be done with sin and not live our earthly lives "for evil human desires, but rather for the will of God" (1 Peter 4:2). No matter how effective we are in our intercultural relationships, when sin creeps into our lives or into the lives of our fellow workers, God removes his blessing and transfers his power and presence to servants who commit to lives of purity and obedience.

Disciples: Agents of Transformation

The transformation of culture occurs when the people of God live in the fear of the Lord and walk in the light of God's Word. The solutions that we create in our cultural systems are feeble, and they are utterly inadequate apart from the power of God working in us. When we place our trust in our systems, we shall certainly fail. Israel's kings led the people into idolatry, war, and ultimately captivity and the destruction of their community. Pastor Samson deemed himself more important than his fellow elders, his mission colleagues, and the ministry of Bible translation with which he had been entrusted. He compromised the integrity of God's Word and held the Scriptures captive to his own selfish desires. His choices led to public rejection of his own work and the undermining of the church of Jesus Christ in his language group. Pastor Absalom in the Midwest Bible Church saw himself as wiser than his elders and certain of the power of his solutions to the growing of a great local church. He insisted upon a plan of action that alienated some members of his congregation while showing favoritism toward others, dividing the church, despising the local community, and leading his people into captivity of a huge mortgage and facility that was far from most of their homes.

Each of these cases shows people of God who in circumstances of trial and challenge turn from faith in God to faith in cultural systems and leaders. When we fear our circumstances, we inevitably fall into idolatry. Samuel reminded the people of Israel that the fear of the Lord, and only the fear of the Lord, leads to obedience, triumph against our enemy, and effectiveness in our service to the king, the Lord Jesus Christ.

A few years ago a missionary named Larry was reflecting on his ministry in East Africa. As he took account of his decade of ministry, he noted that he had engaged in extensive evangelism,

he had planted churches, he had trained leaders, and he had established schools. As he reflected on his years of ministry, he acknowl-
edged in his prayer to the Lord that he had done everything except
what the Lord had asked him to do, to make disciples. Taking
stock of his personal ministry and fearing the Lord, he committed to give the next decade to the task of making disciples.

Trusting the Lord for wisdom to know how to shape that
process, Larry and his wife started discipling the men and
women whom the Lord brought into their lives. They were faithful each year, investing in men and women, teaching them the
Word of God, helping them to lead others to Christ, and then
helping them to make disciples of others. Some of those men
and women completed the discipleship program but did not lead
anyone to Christ or make disciples. However, others responded
in faith, leading others to Christ and beginning the same process
of making disciples that they had experienced.

At the end of that decade, Larry and his wife took stock of
what God had accomplished during that time. More than four-
teen hundred people had committed to a discipling relationship
either under their direction or under the direction of one of their
disciples. These people live in East African cities, towns, and
cultures. They look like their neighbors, dress like them, work
in similar jobs, and participate in the public life of their communities. With regard to social games, they play whatever game
is required of them in their churches and communities.

Yet something about them is different. Many, if not most,
have become serious about following Jesus Christ, studying his
Word, obeying it, and sharing it with others. Although they are
not a distinguished lot, wherever they go they carry the light of
the gospel. Some spread joy and healing among those who suffer; others love their neighbors; many share from their poverty
or wealth; and a few invite anyone who is willing to begin the
journey of becoming a disciple of Jesus Christ. These people are
learning what disciples of Jesus have always found since the day
of Pentecost: they are becoming pilgrims and strangers in their
own lands, and by their obedience to Christ, they are transforming their cultures.

> Blessed are those whose strength is in you,
> who have set their hearts on pilgrimage.

As they pass through the Valley of Baca,
    they make it a place of springs;
    the autumn rains also cover it with pools.
They go from strength to strength,
    till each appears before God in Zion. (Ps. 84:5–7)

References

Adams, Richard N. 1975. *Energy and structure*. Austin: University of Texas Press.

Bennett, David W. 1993. *Metaphors of ministry: Biblical images for leaders and followers*. Grand Rapids: Baker.

Douglas, Mary. 1982. "Cultural bias." In *In the active voice*. London: Routledge and Kegan Paul.

Hiebert, Paul. 1985. "The missiological implications of an epistemological shift." *TSF Bulletin* (May-June): 12–18.

Koop, Gordon, and Sherwood G. Lingenfelter. 1980. *The Deni of western Brazil*. Dallas: Summer Institute of Linguistics Museum of Anthropology.

Kraft, Charles H. 1981. *Christianity in culture*. Maryknoll, N.Y.: Orbis.

Lingenfelter, Sherwood G. 1975. *Yap: Political leadership and culture change in an island society*. Honolulu: University of Hawaii Press.

———. 1996. *Agents of transformation: A guide for effective cross-cultural ministry*. Grand Rapids: Baker.

Lingenfelter, Sherwood G., and Marvin K. Mayers. 1986. *Ministering cross-culturally*. Grand Rapids: Baker.

Mayers, Marvin K. 1987. *Christianity confronts culture*. Grand Rapids: Zondervan.

Murdock, George Peter. 1949. *Social structure*. New York: Macmillan.

Netting, Robert McC., Richard R. Wilk, and Eric J. Arnould. 1984. *Households: Comparative and historical studies of the domestic group*. Berkeley: University of California Press.

Niebuhr, H. Richard. 1951. *Christ and culture*. New York: Harper Torchbooks.

Shanks, Louis. 1987. "Characteristics of Aukan social structure." Paper presented at Biola University, December 18.

Thompson, Michael, Richard Ellis, and Aaron Wildavsky. 1990. *Cultural theory*. Boulder, Colo.: Westview.

Walls, Andrew. 1982. "The gospel as the prisoner and liberator of culture." *Missionalia* 10/3 (November): 93–105.

Scripture Index

Subject Index

academic culture, 70, 144
American culture
   on borrowing, 86
   on family life, 115, 117
   models of ministry, 172
Amish, 157
animists, 157
apostolic leadership, 78–79, 142–43
Aukan culture, 71–74, 131–32, 143
   on authority, 138–39
   on borrowing, 91
   on competition, 100
   on conflict, 156–57
   on exchange, 97–98
   on family life, 119, 121, 122–23
   on labor, 74, 77, 80
authoritarian social game, 30–31,
     32, 35, 57
   and bureaucracy, 138–39
   and conflict, 153
   and family, 117, 119
   and labor, 70, 74, 78
   and power, 135
   and property, 55
authority
   delegated, 134
   domestic, 114–15
   in Javanese church, 130–31
   and power, 132–33
   and skills, 134–36
   and social games, 136, 138–39
autonomy, 30–31, 34, 84

Balzac, Honoré, 91
banishment, 157

bargaining, 117
Bennett, David W., 37, 141, 145
Bible
   on authority, 143–44
   on families, 113, 120–22
   interpretation, 35
   on leadership, 139–40, 141–45
   on social games, 77–78, 79,
     140–41
   on wealth, 60–61
biblical absolutism, 19
borrowing, 90–92
   in American culture, 83–84, 86
   in Deni culture, 86–88
   in Yapese culture, 84–86
Bowman, Bob, 170
bureaucracy, 70, 73–74, 78, 153
business culture, 70, 144–45

Calvin, John, 18
change, 169–70, 171
China Inland Mission, 170
Chinese, on family, 121
church, 39, 49, 81
   as agency of transformation,
     173–75
   as body of Christ, 127–28
   and grid, 46–47
   and group, 47–48
   as new clan, 125
   and social games, 140
   universal, 15
church buildings. See property
community, 23–25, 26, 137
competition, 55, 89, 100

187

Sherwood Lingenfelter is provost, senior vice president, and professor of intercultural studies at Biola University. He is the coauthor (with Marvin Mayers) of *Ministering Cross-Culturally: An Incarnational Model for Personal Relationships.*